THIS WALKER BOOK BELONGS TO:

_____

_____

_____

_____

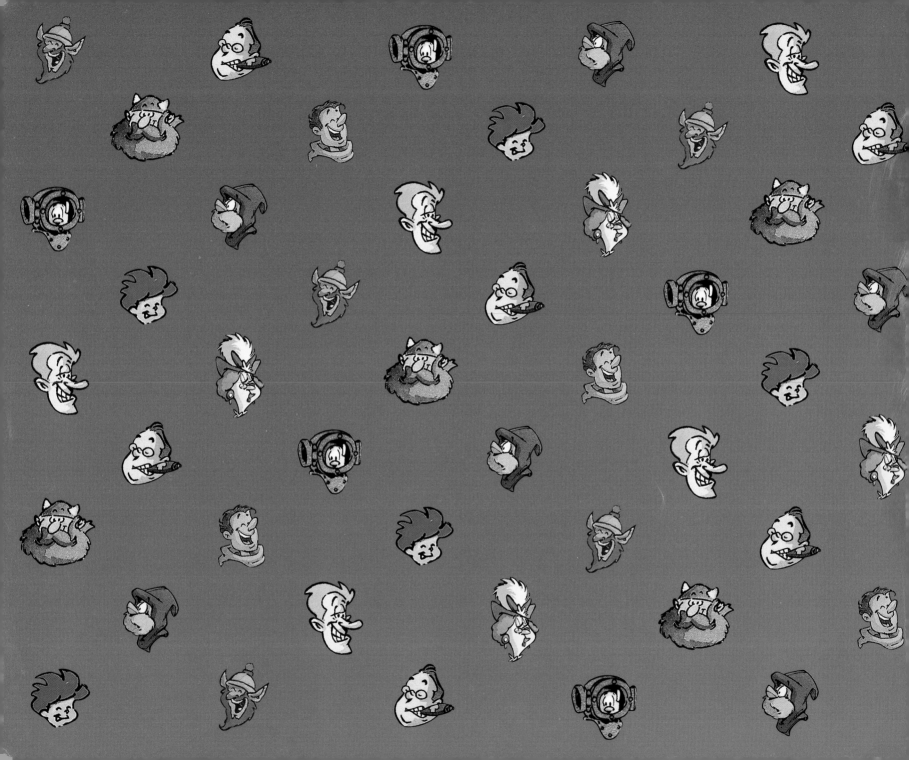

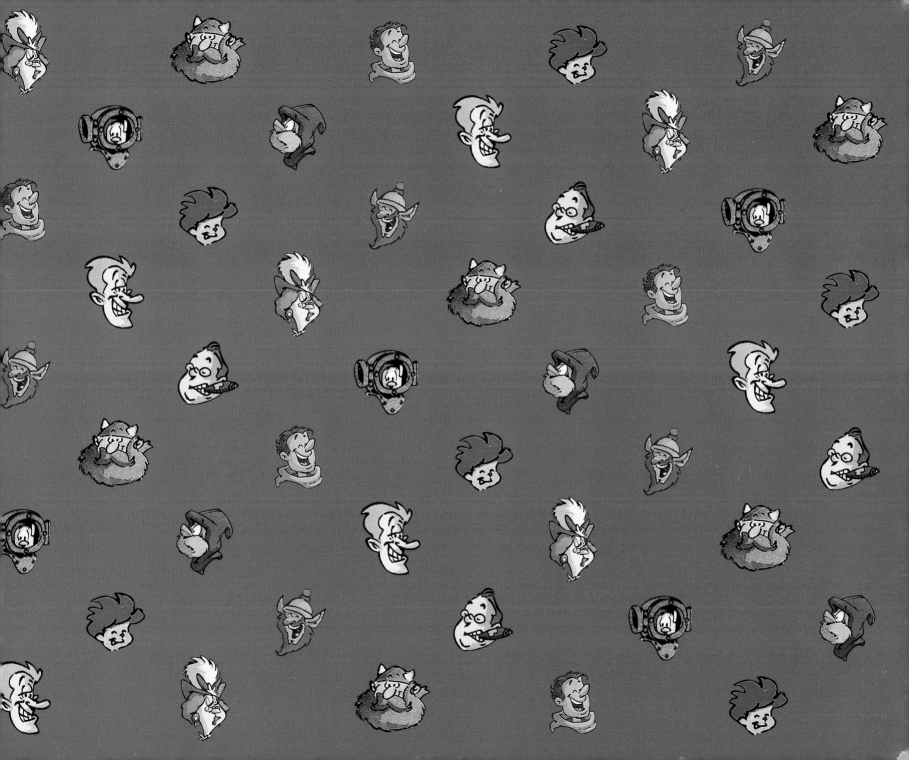

With special thanks to
Stephan Martiniere and Greg Dubuque

This edition published 1999
by Walker Books Ltd, 87 Vauxhall Walk, London SE11 5HJ

First published individually as
Where's Wally? The Wildly Wonderful Activity Book (1994),
Where's Wally? The Simply Sensational Activity Book (1994),
Where's Wally? The Really Remarkable Activity Book (1995) and
Where's Wally? The Completely Crazy Activity Book (1995).

4 6 8 10 9 7 5 3

This book has been typeset in Optima.

Printed in Hong Kong/China

British Library Cataloguing in Publication Data
A catalogue record for this book is available from the British Library.

ISBN 0-7445-6914-1(pb)

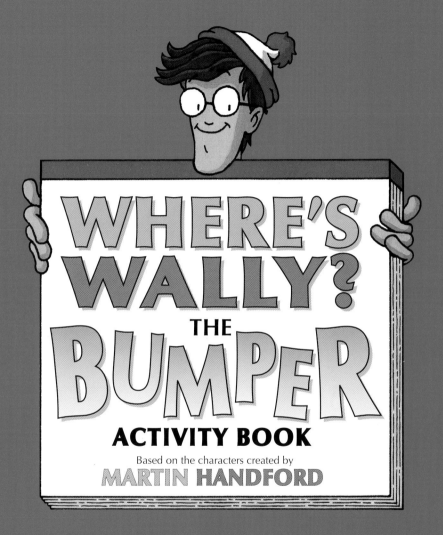

WHERE'S WALLY?
THE BUMPER
ACTIVITY BOOK

Based on the characters created by
MARTIN HANDFORD

WALKER BOOKS
AND SUBSIDIARIES
LONDON · BOSTON · SYDNEY

HI THERE, WALLY-WATCHERS!

I'M OFF ON A FABULOUSLY AMAZING JOURNEY THROUGH THE PAGES OF THIS BUMPER ACTIVITY BOOK. FOLLOW ME INTO THE FUTURE, AND BACK TO THE PAST; FROM UNDER THE SEA TO OUTER SPACE.

AS WELL AS FINDING ME IN EVERY PICTURE, O FAITHFUL FOLLOWERS OF WALLY, THERE ARE AN AMAZING NUMBER OF THINGS TO DO ON THE WAY: GAMES TO PLAY, TONGUE-TWISTERS TO SAY, RIDDLES TO SOLVE AND FACTS TO LEARN. LOOK OUT FOR OUR OLD FRIENDS: YOU SHOULD SEE WOOF 5 TIMES, WENDA 3 TIMES AND WIZARD WHITEBEARD 5 TIMES. BE SURE TO SPOT THAT VILLAIN ODLAW TOO – HE IS LURKING IN 3 PLACES. I WILL LEAVE A STRIPED SOCK AND A SMALL RED AND WHITE WALLY FLAG FOR YOU TO PICK UP. THERE ARE ALSO 17 SCROLLS HIDDEN ALONG THE WAY.

THERE IS ONE MORE TASK TO TELL YOU ABOUT. SOMEWHERE OUTSIDE THE MAIN PICTURE ON EACH PAGE IS A CHARACTER OR OBJECT THAT BELONGS TO ANOTHER SCENE IN THE BOOK. CAN YOU SPOT THE MISFITS AND FIND WHICH PICTURES THEY COME FROM?

THE ANSWERS TO ALL THE RIDDLES AND PUZZLES ARE AT THE BACK, BUT NO CHEATING! AND, IF YOU ARE NOT TOO EXHAUSTED, ALONG THE WAY YOU WILL FIND SOME CHECK LISTS – THERE ARE LOTS OF EXTRA THINGS TO FIND IN EACH PICTURE.

Wally

CARNIVAL CHAOS

DID YOU KNOW?

The first circus was put together by Philip Astley in 1769. He found a diamond ring on Westminster Bridge, sold it and with the money started a trick horse-riding show. He later added a strongman and 2 clowns.

The highest stilts ever walked on were as tall as a 4 storey building.

THINGS TO DO

Crack this code to discover which of all these festive fairground frolics Wally would most like to try out.

ATHES RUPERS WONI ECRO ILLER SCOA ESTER

To solve it, take off the first letter of every set, run all the letters together and see what you've got.

What do you say to a clown with a wooden leg?

Hoppit.

WELL, WANDERERS, THIS IS MY IDEA OF A GOOD DAY OUT – HIDING AMONG THE CROWDS OF A BUSY FUNFAIR. AND I THINK I'LL TAKE ONE OF THESE HOME WITH ME:
MY NOSE IS RED,
MY MOUTH IS WHITE,
IF SHE LETS GO
I'LL DRIFT FROM SIGHT.

CAN YOU GET THIS DART TO LAND ON THE BULL'S EYE OF THE TARGET?

BALL SPORTS

DID YOU KNOW?

There was a game played in Mexico in the tenth century called Po-ta-Pok. It was very like basketball, but if a player managed to shoot the ball through the ring he or she would win all the spectators' clothing!

Basketball players are often very tall. The tallest was Manute Bol who played for the Washington Bullets. He measured 2.30 m.

THINGS TO DO

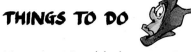

Here are 8 jumbled sports. Can you unjumble them and find the odd one out?

TOLOFABL   SITNEN

STELLABBAK

WIGMINMS   KONORES

FLOG

BEALSLAB   LOVELLYLAB

What does a ball do when it stops rolling?

It looks round.

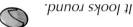

WOW! I'M NOT SURE THESE CRAZY BASKETBALL PLAYERS HAVE QUITE MASTERED ALL THE RULES, BUT THEY'RE HAVING A BALL ANYWAY. THERE ARE SEVERAL UNSUITABLE BITS OF EQUIPMENT ON THE COURT. CAN YOU FIND THIS ONE?
THIS BAT USUALLY HITS A LITTLE WHITE BALL, BUT THE HOLE IN THE MIDDLE IS NO GOOD AT ALL.

WHICH OF THESE BALLS SHOULD NOT BE PLAYED WITH BY HAND?

HI THERE, WIZARD WALLY-HUNTERS, THIS CONJURING SHOW HAS GOT OUT OF HAND. CAN YOU FIND 18 RIOTOUS RABBITS THAT HAVE BEEN PULLED OUT OF THE HAT? AND APART FROM ME, CAN YOU FIND THIS PERSON? SHE LOOKS ALARMED AND WOULDN'T YOU, HER LEGS HAVE LEFT HER IN A BOX SPOTTED BLUE.

WHICH OF THESE SILHOUETTES MATCHES THE MAGICIAN'S BUNNY?

A B C D E

MAGIC MAYHEM

DID YOU KNOW?

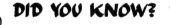

The fastest magician in the world is an American called Dr Eldoonie. He performed 118 different tricks in 2 minutes.

Harry Houdini was famous at the turn of the century for his great feats of escape. In a typical trick he would escape from being chained up and locked in a weighted and roped box that was thrown overboard from a boat. There was no magic involved in his escapes – just physical strength and great agility.

THINGS TO DO

Here's a magic number trick to try on your friends. You might need a calculator.
Pick a 2 digit number (2 different digits, like 84).
Reverse it (48).
Subtract the smaller number from the larger (84 – 48 = 36).
Divide this number by the difference between your original digits (36 ÷ 4). The final answer is always 9.

 *What do you call a space magician?*  :*A flying sorcerer.*

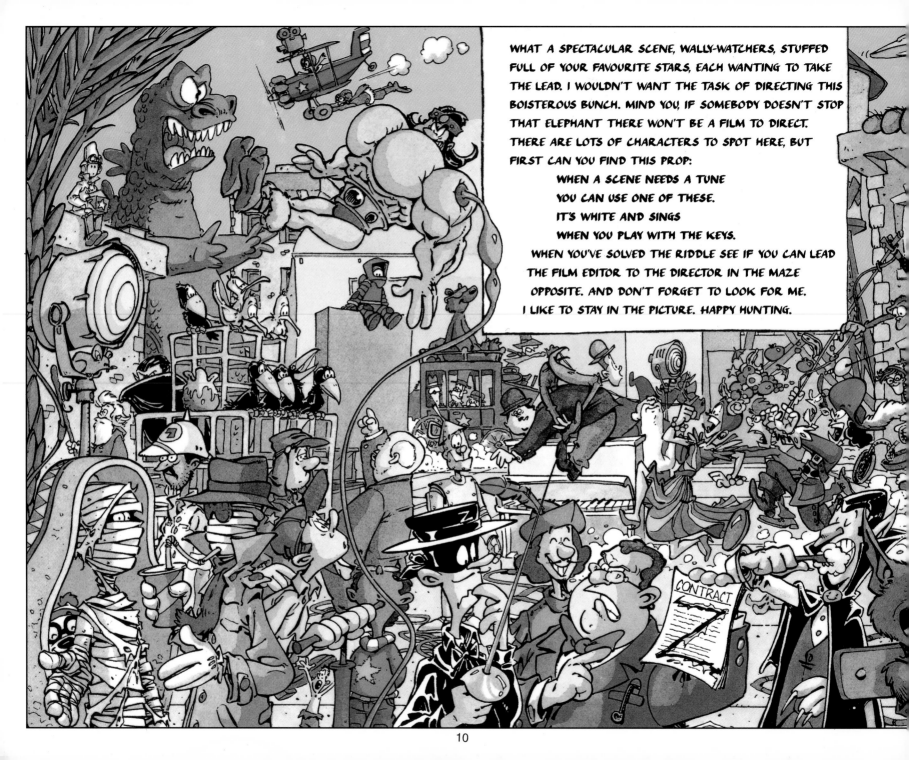

WHAT A SPECTACULAR SCENE, WALLY-WATCHERS, STUFFED FULL OF YOUR FAVOURITE STARS, EACH WANTING TO TAKE THE LEAD. I WOULDN'T WANT THE TASK OF DIRECTING THIS BOISTEROUS BUNCH. MIND YOU, IF SOMEBODY DOESN'T STOP THAT ELEPHANT THERE WON'T BE A FILM TO DIRECT. THERE ARE LOTS OF CHARACTERS TO SPOT HERE, BUT FIRST CAN YOU FIND THIS PROP:

WHEN A SCENE NEEDS A TUNE
YOU CAN USE ONE OF THESE.
IT'S WHITE AND SINGS
WHEN YOU PLAY WITH THE KEYS.

WHEN YOU'VE SOLVED THE RIDDLE SEE IF YOU CAN LEAD THE FILM EDITOR TO THE DIRECTOR IN THE MAZE OPPOSITE. AND DON'T FORGET TO LOOK FOR ME. I LIKE TO STAY IN THE PICTURE. HAPPY HUNTING.

FILM SET

DID YOU KNOW?

Hollywood, in California, became a centre for film making because the weather is nearly always good and there is a wide variety of scenery – from deserts to tropical islands.

The character most often portrayed on film is Sherlock Holmes. The character most often portrayed in horror films is Count Dracula.

The country which has made the most feature films is India.

THINGS TO DO

The names of some famous film characters have been split up. Can you find 5 whole names among these bits? What piece of film-making equipment can you make from the remaining pieces?

BAD   TAR   ALA

DRA   CLA

ZAN   ARD   DDIN

RBO   SIN

CULA   GLI

MOW   PPE

How did Frankenstein eat his food?   *˙uʍop ʇı pǝʇloq ǝH*

MONSTER CARNIVAL

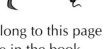

DID YOU KNOW?

The tallest unicycle ever ridden was over 31 m high.

One of the longest journeys ever undertaken on a unicycle was 1450 km, from Land's End to John o' Groats.

THINGS TO DO

Here are 4 pieces of picture. 2 belong to this page and 2 come from somewhere else in the book. Can you find exactly where?

A   B   C   D

Why couldn't the bicycle stand up for itself?

Because it was two-tyred.

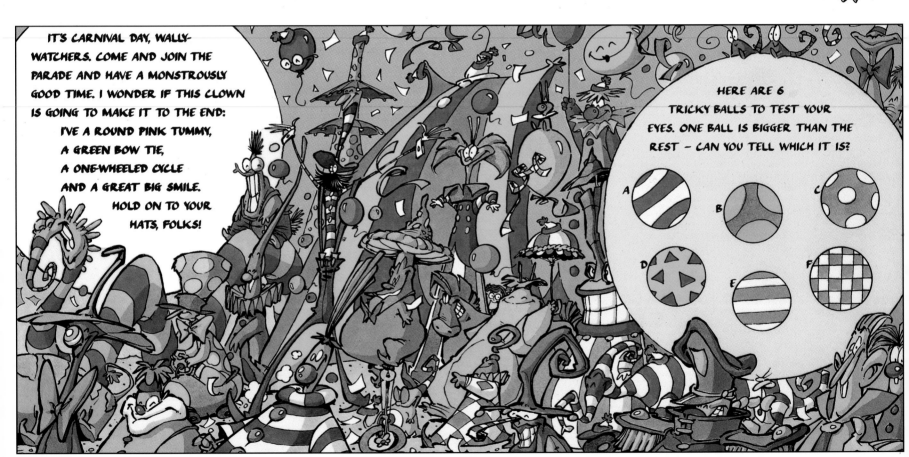

IT'S CARNIVAL DAY, WALLY-WATCHERS. COME AND JOIN THE PARADE AND HAVE A MONSTROUSLY GOOD TIME. I WONDER IF THIS CLOWN IS GOING TO MAKE IT TO THE END:
I'VE A ROUND PINK TUMMY,
A GREEN BOW TIE,
A ONE-WHEELED CYCLE
AND A GREAT BIG SMILE.
HOLD ON TO YOUR
HATS, FOLKS!

HERE ARE 6 TRICKY BALLS TO TEST YOUR EYES. ONE BALL IS BIGGER THAN THE REST – CAN YOU TELL WHICH IT IS?

A   B   C   D   E   F

> I'M SURE EVERY WALLY-WATCHER ENJOYS A GOOD PILLOW FIGHT FROM TIME TO TIME BUT THESE NIGHT-TIME KNIGHTS HAVE TAKEN THINGS A BIT FAR. CAN YOU SEE THIS CHAP WHO IS ALL READY FOR BED?
> HE'S CLEANED HIS TEETH, YOU CAN TELL BY HIS SMILE, THEY'RE GLEAMING AND WHITE AND STAND OUT HALF A MILE.

> YOU'VE HEARD OF COUNTING SHEEP, WELL, TRY COUNTING THESE PILLOWS BELOW AND SEE HOW TIRED IT MAKES YOU.

PILLOW FIGHT PARTY

DID YOU KNOW?

Every night you grow about 8 mm as your spine relaxes. During the day you shrink again!

Some sloths and armadillos spend up to 80 % of their lives asleep.

The largest bed ever built was big enough for 39 people.

THINGS TO DO

What is hidden in this giant bedsock?

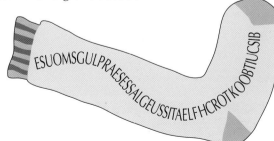

ESUOMSGULPRAESESSALGEUSSITAELFHCROTKOOBTIUCSIB

Why did the man put his bed in the fireplace?

Because he wanted to sleep like a log.

FILM SET FROLICS

DID YOU KNOW?

The first feature film ever was made in Australia in 1906. It was called *The Story of The Kelly Gang*.

1950's America saw the arrival of Smellovision or Aromarama, where appropriate smells were piped into seats during the film.

The biggest cinema in the world is the Radio City Music Hall in New York City. It has 5,874 seats.

THINGS TO DO

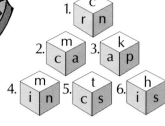

In this puzzle you are looking for 6 six-letter words to do with films. Each sentence below gives you a clue and 3 of the letters can be found in the boxes.

1. A film is shown on one.
2. A film is made with one.
3. Lipstick and powder.
4. A film is shown at one.
5. An actor learns his lines from one.
6. They make sure it's bright enough.

1. c r n
2. m c a
3. k a p
4. m i n 5. t c s 6. h i s

What's on at the cinema every week?

The roof.

I'D BE SURPRISED IF ANY FILMS WERE MADE IN SILLYWOOD STUDIOS, WOULDN'T YOU? AND AS IF THERE WASN'T ENOUGH CHAOS ALREADY, I CAN SEE SOMETHING ABOUT TO CAUSE MORE: IT'S YELLOW AND DANGEROUS DOWN ON THE FLOOR, WHEN THE MAN TAKES A STEP HE'LL GO FLYING FOR SURE.

CAN YOU MATCH THE SILHOUETTES TO THE RIGHT BITS IN THE PICTURE AND FIND THE ODD ONE OUT?

TOYSHOP TROUBLE

DID YOU KNOW?

The teddy bear is named after the American president Theodore "Teddy" Roosevelt, who was once given a real black bear cub.

The biggest teddy bear's picnic ever was attended by 16,837 teds and their owners in 1994.

One of the longest stuffed toys in the world was a snake measuring 312 m.

THINGS TO DO

Eight things from the toyshop are hidden in the letter maze below – 4 across and 4 down. Use the clues to find the across words (we have done one for you), then find the down words. Each letter is used just once.

D B	B **I**	**D** C	**E** K	A cube with spots on
A M	A E	O N	I E	Horse's hair
L F	A O	U L	T R	A number
D L	U R	L C	K E	A yellow quacker

How do you get rid of a boomerang?

Throw it down a one-way street.

15

CARNIVAL CHAOS

- Candyfloss
- Popcorn
- A clown on stilts
- A winning pig
- A grey mouse
- A long red flag
- A pink elephant
- A pair of stripy underpants
- A green flag
- A naughty baby

FILM SET

- Tarzan
- The Tin Man
- Laurel & Hardy
- A flying saucer
- 2 Draculas
- The Invisible Man
- Robin Hood
- Charlie Chaplin
- A red spaceman
- A smiling face badge

PILLOW FIGHT PARTY

- A sleeper on a pole
- 7 white pillows
- A blue soft horse
- A twisted yellow pillow
- 7 red and white nightcaps
- A head in a pillow
- An orange-headed horse
- 2 blue and white nightcaps
- A green cushion
- 9 teddies

BALL SPORTS

- 19 tennis balls
- A broken tennis racket
- 2 striped balloons
- 2 flags
- A twisted golf club
- 4 coloured juggling balls
- 2 pool balls
- An orange balloon
- A huge bowling ball
- A man with a grey beard

FILM SET FROLICS

- A yellow bird
- A piece of cake
- 2 gold coins
- A sleeping man
- 3 men tangled in wires
- An umbrella
- 2 microphones
- A stills photographer
- An elephant
- A guitar

MAGIC MAYHEM

- A yellow and red wand
- 11 juggling balls
- 4 red playing cards
- A wizard in a red hat
- 4 blue playing cards
- 7 top hats
- A yellow bow tie
- A frog
- A sorceress
- 10 white cards

MONSTER CARNIVAL

- A very thin clown
- 3 green buttons
- 2 pairs of glasses
- A striped parasol
- A green balloon
- A blue and white streamer
- Twin monster insects
- A question mark hat
- 10 Wally bobble hats
- A red bow tie

TOYSHOP TROUBLE

- A key
- A wooden block
- A ball on a roller-skate
- A toy with 5 legs
- An alligator on a trapeze
- A bear in a Wally hat
- 3 stripy pencils
- A cow doll
- A happy pig
- 10 Wally dolls

MOON WALKING

DID YOU KNOW?

It would take a car travelling at 60 mph 175 years to reach the sun.

Most planets, including the Earth, spin from west to east, left to right, clockwise, but Venus spins from east to west.

When astronauts are weightless in space their muscles stretch slightly, making them a little taller.

THINGS TO DO

Here are the names of 8 space operations. Can you find them all in the grid?

VOYAGER   APOLLO

ATLANTIS   EXPLORER   MERCURY

SPUTNIK   NASA   DISCOVERY

N	E	V	O	Y	A	G	E	R	I
L	A	N	R	M	S	T	R	O	N
M	G	A	W	A	S	T	H	E	F
E	I	S	R	S	T	M	A	N	O
R	N	A	T	L	A	N	T	I	S
C	D	I	S	C	O	V	E	R	Y
U	T	H	A	P	O	L	L	O	E
R	E	R	O	L	P	X	E	M	O
Y	K	I	N	T	U	P	S	O	N

Read the remaining letters from left to right on every line and you will learn another fascinating space fact.

What do you call a crazy spaceman?

An astronut.

WHAT A WILD BUNCH OF MAD PROFESSORS WE HAVE HERE, WALLY-WATCHERS. THIS IS THE "INSTITUTE-OF-INTERESTING-INVENTIONS-AND-THEIR-EVEN-MORE-INTERESTING-INVENTORS" AND THEY ARE HAVING THEIR ANNUAL CONFERENCE. CAN YOU SEE THE MAN WITH A VACUUM HAT ON HIS HEAD? OR THE INVENTOR WEARING THE LONGEST PAIR OF LEGS YOU'VE EVER SEEN? AND HOW ABOUT THIS FOR A SPECTACULAR DEVELOPMENT?

A WHITE CHICKEN LAID IT
AND LOOK – IT'S BEEN FOUND,
BUT IT'S RATHER UNUSUAL,
IT'S SQUARE AND NOT ROUND.

THERE IS SUPPOSED TO BE A PRIZE FOR THE MOST USEFUL INVENTION AT THE CONVENTION. WHO DO YOU THINK WILL WIN, O FAITHFUL FOLLOWERS? MY FAVOURITE IS THE SUPER-POWERFUL POGO STICK, BUT PERHAPS THE POTION THAT MADE THE INVISIBLE MAN WOULD BE MORE USEFUL. NOT THAT I NEED TO BE INVISIBLE TO BE DIFFICULT TO FIND. CAN YOU SPOT ME IN THIS SCENE?

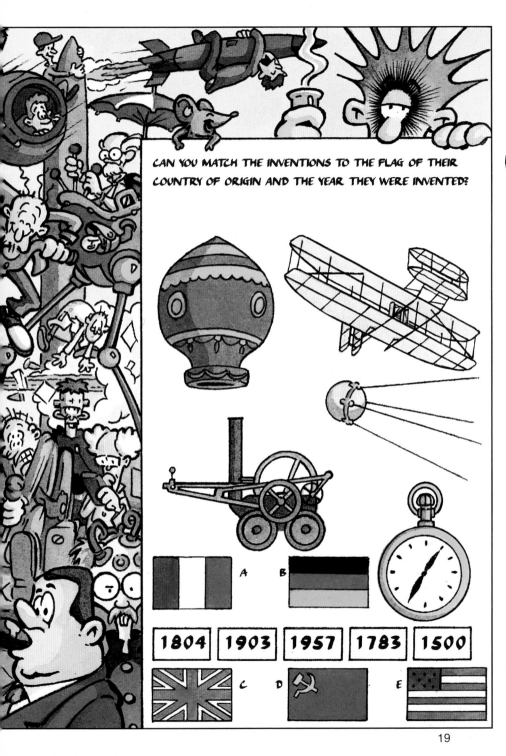

CAN YOU MATCH THE INVENTIONS TO THE FLAG OF THEIR COUNTRY OF ORIGIN AND THE YEAR THEY WERE INVENTED?

A   B

1804 1903 1957 1783 1500

C   D   E

INVENTION CONVENTION

DID YOU KNOW?

The inventor of roller-skates, Joseph Merlin, was a bit of a show-off. At a dinner party in 1760, he skated and played a violin at the same time. He eventually lost control and crashed into a mirror, breaking it and the violin!

Although the tin can was invented in 1812, it took 50 years before someone got round to inventing the label!

The first submarine was made in 1642. It carried 12 men who rowed along underwater using giant oars.

THINGS TO DO

Can you match the silhouettes to the correct part of the picture? Two shapes come from other scenes in the book. Can you work out which ones and where they come from?

What's the world's most useless invention? ˙ǝnlƃ ʞɔıʇs-uoN

STAR GAZING

DID YOU KNOW?

There are trillions of stars in the universe but only 5,780 are visible from Earth without a telescope.

The very centre of a star is extremely hot. It can reach a temperature of 16 million °C.

The longest name of any star is *Shurnarkabishashututu*. It is Arabic for "under the southern horn of the bull".

THINGS TO DO

Here is a martian signpost. Can you work out what it says by using the code-breaker? Read the grid across first then up to get each letter.

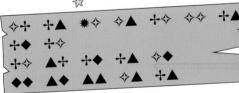

	A	B	C	D	E
▲	A	B	C	D	E
✳	F	G	H	I	J
✧	K	L	M	N	O
◆	P	Q	R	S	T
✛	U	V	W	X	Y/Z

What's a spaceman's favourite game? *Astronaughts and crosses.*

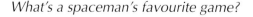

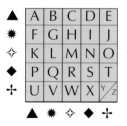

CONSTRUCTION CHAOS

DID YOU KNOW?

Skyscrapers are designed to be flexible so that if the wind gets very strong the building will sway and not snap. In earthquake zones skyscrapers are built on rubber springs, so that they bounce with the shakes.

The Great Pyramid of Cheops is the world's largest stone building. The cathedrals of St Peter's, Florence, Milan, St Paul's and Westminster Abbey would all fit into its base alone.

THINGS TO DO

In this puzzle you are looking for 6 six-letter words to do with building. Each sentence below gives you a clue and 3 of the letters are in the word bricks.

1. Bricks are fixed together with this.
2. Nails are bashed in with this.
3. A glass-filled hole in a wall.
4. Long, thin pieces of wood.
5. A stone column.
6. Useful for climbing up.

What do you get if you cross a cement mixer with a hen? A bricklayer.

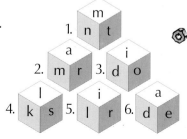

WOW! WOOF AND I ARE HAVING A GREAT TIME SPEEDING THROUGH THE STRATOSPHERE ON OUR SUPER SUPERSONIC SPACE SAUCER. IT'S GOOD TO KNOW THERE IS LIFE BEYOND THE STARS, EVEN THOUGH IT MIGHT BE A BUNCH OF CRAZY ALIENS.

I'M STARTING TO FEEL DIZZY FROM GOING SO FAST. PERHAPS WE COULD DROP IN TO THE ALIEN CAFE FOR A GLASS OF MARTIAN LEMONADE AND AN ASTRO-BURGER, BUT IT LOOKS LIKE A POPULAR PLACE AND WE'LL HAVE TO JOIN THE QUEUE. CAN YOU SPOT THIS FELLOW WHO HAS ALREADY PAID A VISIT?

I FORGOT I WAS WEIGHTLESS
WHEN I LEFT THE GROUND,
AND I LOST SOMETHING NICE
AS I FLOATED AROUND.

HELP THIS MARTIAN PICK UP A BURGER AND LEMONADE AND TAKE THEM TO HIS FRIEND.

FLYING SAUCERS

DID YOU KNOW?

People have been spotting UFOs (Unidentified Flying Objects) since the thirteenth century.

Most UFOs can be explained away as clouds or reflections from stars, but not all of them. In 1971 2 Americans claimed to have been captured and examined by aliens on board a UFO.

THINGS TO DO

A constellation is a group of stars which form a shape in the sky. Can you find the names of 6 constellations below?

CORVUSTAURUSCYGNUSLEOURSAMAJORORION

How can you see flying saucers?

Trip up the waiter.

LIGHT FANTASTIC

DID YOU KNOW?

The light bulb was invented by Thomas Edison
in 1879. Edison was responsible for lots of inventions,
including a gramophone, a megaphone
and a sewing machine that was run
by the sound of a human voice.

1 square centimetre of the sun's surface
is as bright as the light on 232,500 candles.

Each bulb at the top of the Empire State Building gives out
the light of 450 million candles.

THINGS TO DO

The vanishing stamp trick
Here is a trick of the light. Put a postage stamp face up on the table.
Put a glass of water on top of the stamp and a plate on top of the
glass. Look into the glass from any angle and you will see that the
stamp has disappeared.

 What would you use if you swallowed a light bulb?

 A candle.

24

RAMSHACKLE ROBOTS

DID YOU KNOW?

The word "robot" comes from the Czech word *robota*, meaning "forced labour". It was first used to describe a mechanical man by a Czech playwright called Karel Capek in 1923.

The world's smallest moving robot is tinier than a sugar cube.

A steam-driven pigeon robot was made in Ancient Greece almost 2,000 years ago.

THINGS TO DO

In this robot-code, all the letters have a different number value and each word has the value of the letters added together.

Here's a clue:

H = 8, A = 7, T = 5

so the word HAT is 8 + 7 + 5 = 20.

Look at the code-grid and work out the value of the word ROBOT.

$$
\begin{array}{ccccccc}
R & + & B & + & T & = & 9 \\
+ & & + & & + & & \\
0 & + & 0 & + & 0 & = & 6 \\
+ & & + & & + & & \\
0 & + & R & + & 0 & = & 7 \\
= & & = & & = & & \\
7 & & 6 & & 9 & &
\end{array}
$$

Why was the robot being silly? Because he had a screw loose.

RATTLING RUSTBUCKETS! THINGS ARE GETTING A LITTLE OVER-CROWDED IN ROBOT CITY. THESE METAL MARVELS COME IN ALL SHAPES AND SIZES BUT THIS ONE IS THE STRANGEST OF ALL:

THIS ROBOT IS BROKEN, HIS HEAD'S JUST SPLIT WIDE, BUT SOMEONE QUITE STARTLING IS HIDING INSIDE.

THIS ROBOT IS MADE UP OF 7 PARTS OF ROBOTS IN THE PICTURE AND 1 PART ALL HIS OWN — <u>WHICH</u> PIECE IS IT?

THE TREMENDOUS TECHNOLOGY CHECK LIST
Lots more things for Wally-watchers to look for.

STAR GAZING
- 19 yellow stars
- A cup and saucer
- 2 buckets
- A 4-eyed creature
- An astronaut sitting on a sign
- A crash-landing
- An octopus
- A family of yellow bugs
- A space garage
- A spoon

LIGHT FANTASTIC
- A desk lamp hat
- 2 yellow headlamps
- A yellow Chinese lantern
- A man in a Wally lampshade
- An Aladdin's lamp
- A breaking fluorescent tube
- A pair of square glasses
- A brown book
- 9 candles
- 8 smiling light bulbs

MOON WALKING
- 2 dogs in spacesuits
- A magnifying glass
- A pancake being tossed
- A chicken in a spacesuit
- A fish in a spacesuit
- 2 butterfly nets
- A snake in a spacesuit
- 3 smiling stars
- A satellite dish
- A baseball

CONSTRUCTION CHAOS
- A sculptor
- A rhino on a crane
- A tin can
- A saw
- A demolition ball
- A man with a blowtorch
- A sleep-worker
- A man eating his lunch
- A sausage
- 3 mice

INVENTION CONVENTION
- 7 light bulbs
- An invisible man
- A giant mouse
- A baby's bottle
- A man on a pogo stick
- A green cup
- A dancing robot
- A magnet
- A shrinking man
- A mouse in a glass case

RAMSHACKLE ROBOTS
- A goldfish
- A can of oil
- A robot with a radio
- A red flag
- A bug in a stripy shirt
- A robot dog
- A robot washing-line
- 2 red arrows
- A helicopter robot
- 8 tin cans

FLYING SAUCERS
- A man with 6 arms
- A green cat
- A flower
- 3 teacups
- 3 milk bottles
- A dog in a spacesuit
- A piece of cheese
- A cat in a spacesuit
- A slice of cake
- 3 mice

SHOPPING SPREE

DID YOU KNOW?

The first supermarket was opened in 1916 in Memphis, Tennessee in America. It was called the Piggly Wiggly store!

The largest cheese ever weighed over 18 kg.

In 1989 a team of workers built a whole stadium out of two million empty tin cans. It took 18,000 hours.

THINGS TO DO

Crack the code and find out what Wally was looking for in the shop. The first letter is underlined.

2 cakes
1 biscuit
3 onions
5 oranges

5 apricots
2 sherberts
4 lemons
5 apricots
4 lemons
4 apples
2 cakes
3 potatoes
7 sausages

5 apricots
2 cakes
7 haddock
7 sausages

What's the study of shopping called?   Buy-ology.

WOW! WHAT A BUNCH OF CRAZY SHOPPERS. IT LOOKS AS IF THEY'LL SHOP TILL THEY DROP. CAN YOU SPOT WHAT THIS MAN WANTS TO BUY? I'M WEARING A GAS MASK, THOUGH I NEED JUST A SLICE. IT'S DELICIOUS ON BREAD AND A FAVOURITE WITH MICE.

CAN YOU SPOT 9 DIFFERENCES BETWEEN THESE BOXES OF SHOPPING?

A FEAST OF PIES

DID YOU KNOW?

The biggest cake ever made weighed over 58 tonnes, including 7.35 tonnes of icing.

The oldest cake in the world is over 4,000 years old. It was vacuum-packed in an Egyptian grave in 2200 BC.

The longest loaf of bread ever made was 718.67 m long.

THINGS TO DO

Model your own Wally face by using this recipe to make salt dough:
Mix together 100g plain flour, 150g salt, a dessertspoon of cooking oil and enough water to make a stretchy dough. Knead it until smooth and shape your model. Bake the dough in a cool oven for 2 – 3 hours until hard. When it is quite cold, colour your model with paints or felt-tip pens. This is not an edible recipe!

What looks just like half a loaf of bread? ʇlɐɥ ɹǝɥʇo ǝɥ┴

28

FABULOUS FOOD

DID YOU KNOW?

The largest ever continuous sausage was made in England in 1988 and measured 21.12 km.

The biggest tomato on record weighed 3.51 kg.

The stems and leaves of a tomato plant are toxic and could make you extremely ill if you ate them.

THINGS TO DO

Here are 6 fruit and vegetable circle puzzles. To solve each one start at any corner and read clockwise or anticlockwise.

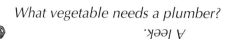

R O O	C R E	M A T	M M O	T A T	S H E
T T	U B	O O	U O	O O	I S
E E B	C U M	T S E	S H R	P S E	D A R

Which of these can be seen in the picture?

What vegetable needs a plumber?

A leek.

HERE IS A FABULOUS FANTASY FOR ANY FAMISHED WALLY-WATCHERS, BUT EVEN IF YOU FIND SOMETHING TASTY IT IS QUITE LIKELY TO GET UP AND WALK OFF YOUR PLATE. CAN YOU SPOT THIS SHY VEGETABLE?
IT'S TRYING TO HIDE
BUT IS EASILY SEEN,
IT'S ORANGE AND POPULAR
AT HALLOWE'EN.

IN ALL THIS CHAOS SOMEONE HAS BROKEN A PLATE. MOST BITS HAVE BEEN STUCK BACK TOGETHER BUT CAN YOU FIND THE LAST 2 PIECES FROM THE 4 BELOW?

CREAM OF THE CAKES

DID YOU KNOW?

One of the largest chocolate chip cookies ever made contained over 3 million chocolate chips.

The word "cookie" comes from the Dutch word "koekje" which means "little cake".

It is almost impossible to eat a sugary doughnut all up without licking your lips. Try it!

THINGS TO DO

These 5 doughnuts look tasty, but they are filled with some pretty strange ingredients. To work out each one, start at any corner and read clockwise or anticlockwise.

What jumps from tree to tree and tastes of almonds? Tarzipan.

ICE-CREAM PARTY

DID YOU KNOW?

The Chinese probably invented ice-cream. They used to eat snow mixed with lemons, oranges or pomegranates.

The record for ice-cream eating is over 9 litres in 8 minutes.

The largest ice-cream ever was a sundae made in Canada in 1988. It weighed nearly 25 kg, including syrup and topping.

THINGS TO DO

Here are 4 favourite pudding combinations. The first parts are given, but three letter clues to the second parts are written in the cubes. Can you work out what the complete puddings are?

Strawberries and [c / r / a]   Pancakes and [r / s / p]

Jelly and [m / c / e]   Bananas and [a / s / d]

How does a monster count to 19?   *On his fingers.*

THESE ICE-CREAM LOVERS ARE TRYING TO WORK OUT WHICH COMBINATION OF FLAVOURS THEY ALL LIKE THE BEST.
A LONG YELLOW FRUIT THAT'S EASY TO SLICE, PLUS FINE ORANGE JAM THAT ON TOAST IS QUITE NICE.

CAN YOU UNJUMBLE THE UNUSUAL ICE-CREAM FLAVOURS ON THESE BOTTLES?

SPAR PIN

LICOROBC

TAM OTO

GEBACAB

RAC TOR

VEGETABLE MATTERS

DID YOU KNOW?

Potatoes were eaten in South America as long ago as 200 AD.

The durian, a fruit from south-east Asia, is the world's smelliest fruit, but it is also very delicious.

Tomatoes were first eaten as fruit, and not used like vegetables until the 19th century.

THINGS TO DO

The Great Fruit and Veg Maze

Hidden in this maze are 3 fruit and vegetables which have been split into two. Match up the halves, shading in the boxes as you do so. Then trace a path through the maze using just the shaded letters. Which letter do you come to?

A

	ape		
on	ato	ana	
START ▶	pot	let	ple	ear	▶ B
par	eek	ion	

C

What's round, brown and giggles?

A tickled onion.

WOW! I HAD NO IDEA FRUIT AND VEGETABLES COULD HAVE SO MUCH FUN, DID YOU FRIENDS? CAN YOU FIND THIS STYLISH FELLOW SOMEWHERE IN THE PICTURE. MY MOUTH IS WIDE OPEN, THERE'S A CURL ON MY HEAD, I'M WEARING DARK GLASSES MY COLOUR IS RED.

THREE OF THESE ARE FRUIT. WHICH ONES?

EASTER PARADE

DID YOU KNOW?

The Easter bunny was originally the hare, which was linked to pagan spring festivals and the moon goddess.

The longest rabbit ears found were 71 cm long.

A single pair of rabbits could produce a family of 33 million animals in only 3 years if all their offspring survived.

THINGS TO DO

There are more words than you might expect hidden in an:

EASTER BUNNY

How many can you find?

20, good;
30, very good;
over 50, really remarkable!

What do you call a naughty egg?

A practical yolker.

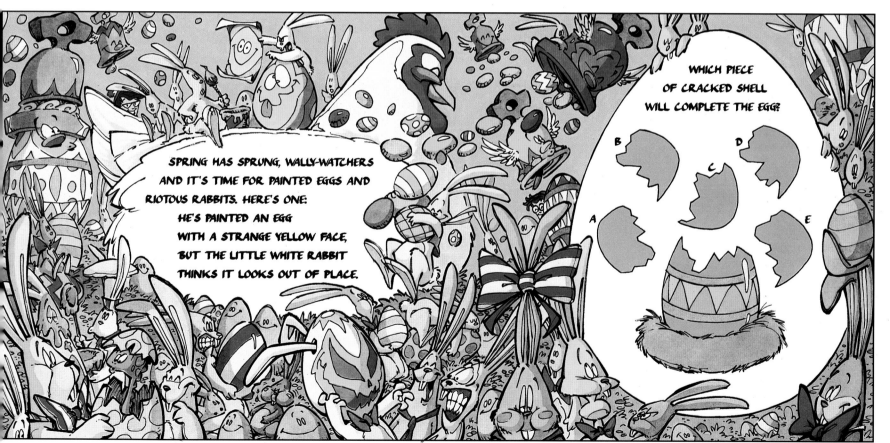

SPRING HAS SPRUNG, WALLY-WATCHERS AND IT'S TIME FOR PAINTED EGGS AND RIOTOUS RABBITS. HERE'S ONE: HE'S PAINTED AN EGG WITH A STRANGE YELLOW FACE, BUT THE LITTLE WHITE RABBIT THINKS IT LOOKS OUT OF PLACE.

WHICH PIECE OF CRACKED SHELL WILL COMPLETE THE EGG?

COOKING COMPETITION

DID YOU KNOW?

The red food colouring cochineal is made from the dried bodies of small South American insects.

Cheese was used as a medicine in Ancient Greece.

According to legend, King Alfred the Great got into trouble when he forgot to keep an eye on a peasant woman's cakes in the oven and let them burn!

THINGS TO DO

The Amazing Biscake (half biscuit, half cake!)

You will need: 75 g sugar, 75 g butter, 1 tbsp drinking chocolate, an egg, a 300 g packet of crisp tea biscuits.

1. Put the biscuits in a plastic bag and crush using a rolling-pin.
2. Beat the egg in a bowl and put it into a saucepan with the sugar, drinking chocolate and butter. Melt over a low heat and keep stirring until the mixture boils. Then take it off the heat.
3. Add the biscuits, mix and leave to cool.
4. Mould the mixture into any shape you like. Put it in the fridge to get really cold and then eat it!

Why are cooks cruel?   *Because they whip cream and beat eggs.*

SILLY SWEETS

DID YOU KNOW?

The largest sweet ever was a marzipan chocolate which weighed as much as 24 people.

Americans chew enough gum every year to make a single stick 8 million km long.

A tooth left overnight in a glass of cola will have dissolved by the morning.

Peppermint Creams

1. Sift 450 g icing sugar into a bowl.
2. Separate an egg white from the yolk and whisk it with a fork.
3. Add the egg white to the icing sugar with 1 tsp peppermint flavouring, then gradually add the juice of one lemon so that you can make a ball of dough with your hands.
4. Sprinkle icing sugar on your surface and roll out the paste. Then cut out delicious peppermint sweets in whatever shapes you like.

How do you stop a lolly slipping out of your mouth?   Grit your teeth.

35

THE FANTASTIC FOOD CHECK LIST
Lots more things for Wally-watchers to look for.

SHOPPING SPREE

- 11 red apples
- 7 bananas
- A boy eating chocolate
- 2 thermometers
- A yellow and white scarf
- A pillow
- A pink bow
- An octopus
- 2 pairs of square glasses
- A baby's bottle

CREAM OF THE CAKES

- 2 flying biscuits
- A biscuit with a moustache
- A greedy green sweet
- A Napoleon éclair
- An éclair lying down
- An éclair with icing buttons
- Cakes on a cloud
- A huge pink éclair
- 2 blue buttons
- A crying cake

EASTER PARADE

- A bunny with tied ears
- A green egg with white spots
- A red and white egg
- A swallowed egg
- 6 red bow ties
- A chef bunny
- A dinosaur egg
- An egg mask
- A sleeping bunny
- 4 flying bells

A FEAST OF PIES

- A chipped plate
- A green bowl
- 6 red neck-scarves
- A flying flan tin
- A yellow neck-scarf
- 22 cherries
- A green neck-scarf
- A cake slice
- A blue saucer
- 3 striped tablecloths

ICE-CREAM PARTY

- 6 ice-cream cornets
- A sleeping pig
- A spanner
- A screwdriver
- A boot
- A long fork
- A checked hanky
- A furry spaceman
- An empty bottle
- A glass of chocolate milk

COOKING COMPETITION

- A twin-headed monster
- A very hot cake
- A carrot cake
- An outer-space cake
- 7 little frogs
- An explorer
- A cross girl
- 4 balloons
- A giant mouse
- 7 cherries with stalks

FABULOUS FOOD

- 2 cherry cakes
- The chef
- A candle
- 3 carrots
- A bone
- A string of sausages
- 6 forks
- A banana
- A pickled gherkin
- A salt cellar

VEGETABLE MATTERS

- A pot of tomato chutney
- A bean necklace
- A stick of celery
- A prune
- A pineapple
- 3 purple grapes
- A banana removing its skin
- A Wally scarf
- 16 green peas
- A pumpkin

SILLY SWEETS

- A greedy pink sweet
- An angry chocolate bean
- 2 red and white walking-sticks
- A red balloon
- 7 flying sweets
- A green lollipop
- 2 red and white lollipops
- A sweet with pink lips
- 13 jellybean people
- A yellow bear

WATER WONDERLAND

DID YOU KNOW?

Some seaweeds produce a sticky substance called alginic acid which helps them hold on to rocks. We add it to ice-cream to stop it separating.

The earliest submarines were powered by steam and got very hot under the water.

One of the first submarines was used in 1776, during the American Civil War. It was called The Turtle.

THINGS TO DO

The message Wally has to find is written in code. Decode it by writing each set of letters down backwards.

LAWOT CODYL OTEMO OLAET TCOEV SUPO

Why did the crab blush?   *Because the seaweed.*

ONE GLIMPSE OF THE SUN AND EVERYONE'S OUT FOR SOME SENSATIONAL SEASIDE FUN. THIS PLACE IS SO POPULAR EVEN THE DOLPHINS HAVE TO QUEUE UP TO SWIM. CAN YOU SEE EMERALDA, THE GREEN FOREST WOMAN, HAVING A WHALE OF A TIME, AND WHAT ABOUT THE CRAZY MAN DRIVING HIS JET-SKI UP THE WAVE?

I'M HAVING A SWELL TIME, BUT I'M NOT SURE THIS FURRY FRIEND ENJOYS THE WATER:

I'M HERE ON THE ROLLERS
BY DRACULA LED,
I'D MUCH RATHER BE
AT HOME IN YOUR BED.

HERE IS A COLLECTION OF THINGS THAT WALLY FOUND ON THE BEACH. CAN YOU SPOT WHICH 2 OBJECTS ARE THE ODD ONES OUT?

SURFER'S PARADISE

DID YOU KNOW?

The first recorded surfer was Lt James King, who surfed off Hawaii Island in 1779.

It is possible to ride a wave for 1700 m in Matancha Bay, Mexico.

About 70% of the world's total surface is covered by water.

THINGS TO DO

Get from one ocean to another by following the instructions:

Start with	A T L A N T I C
Change all Ts to Is	_ _ _ _ _ _ _ _
Change both As to Cs	_ _ _ _ _ _ _ _
Remove the first I	_ _ _ _ _ _ _
Make the first C a P	_ _ _ _ _ _ _
Change the L to an A	_ _ _ _ _ _ _
Swap the N and the first I	_ _ _ _ _ _ _
Change the N to an F	_ _ _ _ _ _ _

What's the best cure for seasickness? Bolt your food down.

IF THESE DIVERS THINK THEY'RE
GOING TO GET HOME WITH LOTS OF LONG
LOST TREASURE THEY'VE GOT ANOTHER THING
COMING – THE SEA CREATURES ARE DOING WHAT
THEY CAN TO STOP THEM AND HAVING GREAT FUN AT
THE SAME TIME. LOOK AT THIS HAPPY ANIMAL:

I'M HIGH ON A LEDGE,
I'M SMILING AND BROWN,
IF I GRAB HIS LONG AIR PIPE
THIS DIVER WILL FROWN.

CAN YOU FIND ME IN MY UNDERWATER GEAR,
WALLY-WATCHERS?

CAN YOU PUT THESE THINGS FROM THE PICTURE INTO 5 RELATED PAIRS?

WHAT A WRECK!

DID YOU KNOW?

The oldest shipwreck ever found was a Bronze Age ship over 3,000 years old.

The Spanish Armada, which attacked Britain in 1588, was thought to be invincible. By the time it returned home, 70 of its 130 ships had been sunk, mostly because of bad weather.

The deepest part of the ocean is the Mariana's Trench in the Pacific. It is 10,916 m deep, which is the depth of 28 Empire State Buildings on top of each other.

THINGS TO DO

Here is a map of the old wreck. There are 7 treasures inside but also a SHARK, an OCTOPUS, a JELLYFISH and a CRAB. Only the crab is safe to go near. Which three treasures can you bring out of the wreck, if you can't go in the rooms with the dangerous creatures?

The treasures are: PEARLS, SWORD, KEY, CHEST, GEM, COINS, RING.

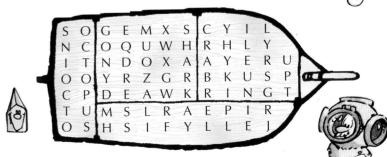

What do you call a baby crab?

A nipper.

POOLSIDE PARADISE

DID YOU KNOW?

The Romans used to wear leather bikinis.

Tarzan actor Johnny Weismuller won 5 Olympic gold medals for swimming. He built a home in Hollywood with a swimming-pool all round it!

The largest swimming-pool in the world is 5 times larger than a football pitch.

THINGS TO DO

After the pool was drained, 6 things were found at the bottom. Work out what they were by matching the right missing letters to add to the boxes.

| wtch | bnn | bt | sndwch | wg | trnks |

aaa   u   a   i   oo   ai

Where do ghouls most like to swim?

Off the South Ghost.

WHAT A LOT OF HAPPY HOLIDAY-MAKERS! AND I'M HERE TOO SOMEWHERE, ENJOYING THE SUN AND FUN. TALKING OF FUN, CAN YOU FIND THIS CHARACTER? I HOPE HE KNOWS WHAT HE'S DOING:

HE'S GOT 6 SHINY BUTTONS AND A TRAY IN HIS HAND;
A SKATEBOARD,
      A RUBBER RING,
WHERE WILL HE LAND?

FIND WHERE EACH OF THESE PIECES COMES FROM IN THE PICTURE AND SPOT THE ONLY ONE THAT MATCHES EXACTLY.

A
B
C
D
E
F

BEACH DELIGHTS

DID YOU KNOW?

Polynesian islanders believed the sound you heard if you put a seashell to your ear was the voice of a god living inside.

A giant clam contains enough meat to provide a meal for 4 people.

 Only 1 oyster in 1,000 actually contains a pearl and it takes 6 years for a pearl to form.

THINGS TO DO

Find your way from sea to sun by following the clues to each word and changing one letter each time.

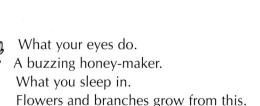

What your eyes do.
A buzzing honey-maker.
What you sleep in.
Flowers and branches grow from this.
A hot cross cake.

SEA
_ _ _
_ _ _
_ _ _
_ _ _
_ _ _
SUN

 What is the best day to go to the beach?

 Sun-day.

43

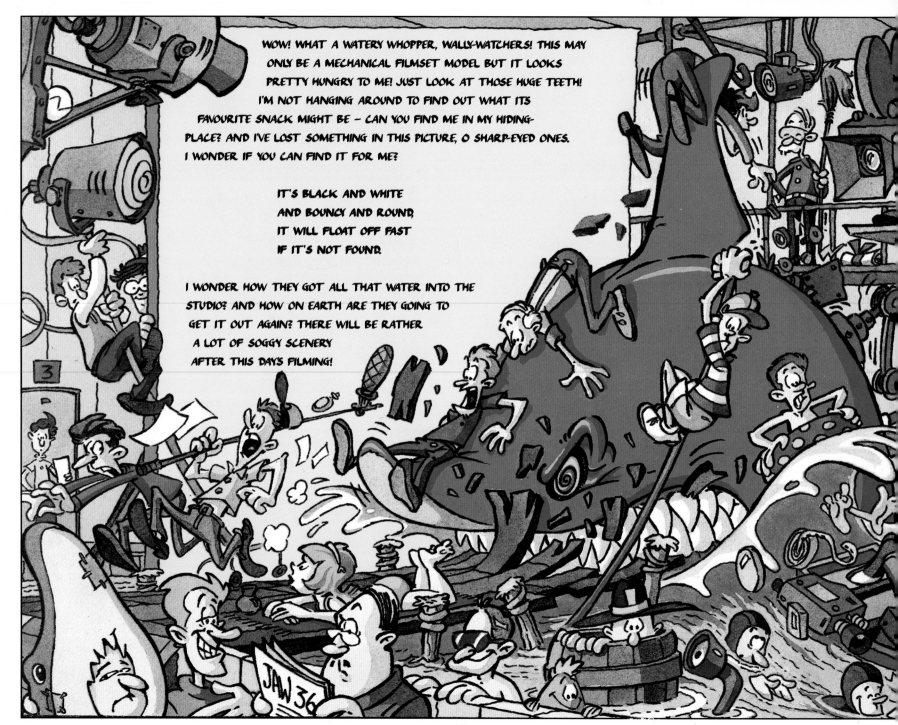

WOW! WHAT A WATERY WHOPPER, WALLY-WATCHERS! THIS MAY ONLY BE A MECHANICAL FILMSET MODEL BUT IT LOOKS PRETTY HUNGRY TO ME! JUST LOOK AT THOSE HUGE TEETH! I'M NOT HANGING AROUND TO FIND OUT WHAT ITS FAVOURITE SNACK MIGHT BE – CAN YOU FIND ME IN MY HIDING-PLACE? AND I'VE LOST SOMETHING IN THIS PICTURE, O SHARP-EYED ONES. I WONDER IF YOU CAN FIND IT FOR ME?

IT'S BLACK AND WHITE
AND BOUNCY AND ROUND,
IT WILL FLOAT OFF FAST
IF IT'S NOT FOUND.

I WONDER HOW THEY GOT ALL THAT WATER INTO THE STUDIO? AND HOW ON EARTH ARE THEY GOING TO GET IT OUT AGAIN? THERE WILL BE RATHER A LOT OF SOGGY SCENERY AFTER THIS DAY'S FILMING!

SHARK SHAMBLES

DID YOU KNOW?

Although the Great White shark is scary enough at 4 m long, this is nothing compared with the ferocious prehistoric Megalodon shark, which was 3 times as big!

A shark's teeth last on average for only 8–10 days. New teeth constantly grow to replace broken ones.

A shoal of vicious piranha in the Amazon can reduce a human to a skeleton in 60 seconds.

Shark skin is so rough it is used as sandpaper in Japan.

THINGS TO DO

Here are 10 types of shark. Can you find them all in the grid?

BULL

NURSE

MAKO THRESHER

TIGER WHALE

LEMON

HAMMERHEAD

BASKING

GREAT WHITE

B	D	O	R	E	G	I	T	L	P	L	H
U	G	R	E	A	T	W	H	I	T	E	I
L	N	N	S	S	O	M	R	E	T	M	I
L	I	M	E	S	G	A	E	N	G	O	U
O	K	A	M	P	O	E	S	R	U	N	N
A	S	S	H	E	L	A	H	W	A	R	K
A	A	N	D	A	T	T	E	A	C	K	I
T	B	H	A	M	M	E	R	H	E	A	D

Read the remaining letters from left to right on every line and learn another toothy fact!

Where do you weigh whales? At the whale-weigh station.

CAN YOU PUT THE CORRECT PIECES OF FISH TOGETHER TO GET 3 WHOLE ONES?

HERE'S A SCENE FOR ALL WATER-LOVERS – ANIMAL AND HUMAN ALIKE. I'M NOT SURE WHAT'S GOING TO HAPPEN WHEN THAT HIPPO LANDS BUT I'M GLAD I'M KEEPING WELL OUT OF THE WAY. AND HERE'S ANOTHER FELLOW WHO'S UP TO NO GOOD:

HE'S RIGHT IN THE MIDDLE
AND HOLDING A PIN,
HE'S PLEASED WITH HIMSELF,
JUST LOOK AT HIM GRIN.

AND TALKING OF TROUBLE-MAKERS, CAN YOU SPOT THE NAUGHTY LITTLE BOY PUTTING VICIOUS CRABS INTO THE POOL? I THINK IT'S TIME THE LIFEGUARD BLEW THE WHISTLE ON HIM AND HIS CRAFTY CRUSTACEANS, BEFORE THEY CAUSE ANY MORE CHAOS.

TWELVE THINGS HAVE BEEN CHANGED IN THIS SCENE FROM THE POOL PICTURE. CAN YOU SPOT THEM?

WACKY WATER FUN

DID YOU KNOW?

Sperm whales can stay underwater for nearly 2 hours before coming up to breathe.

 The Crown of Thorns starfish can eat 34 m² of coral a day.

The largest crocodile in the world is the Saltwater croc, which can grow up to 7 m long – that's about the same as 4 people lying end to end.

THINGS TO DO

Here are 5 jumbled creatures who all spend a good deal of time in and around the water. Can you unjumble them and find 2 pairs and an odd one out?

NUGINEP

ENOLIAS

TRETO

LESGALU

TRALOGILA

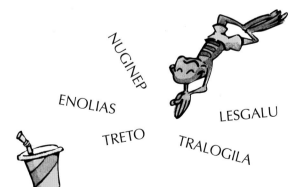

When do your swimming trunks go ding-dong?

When you wring them out.

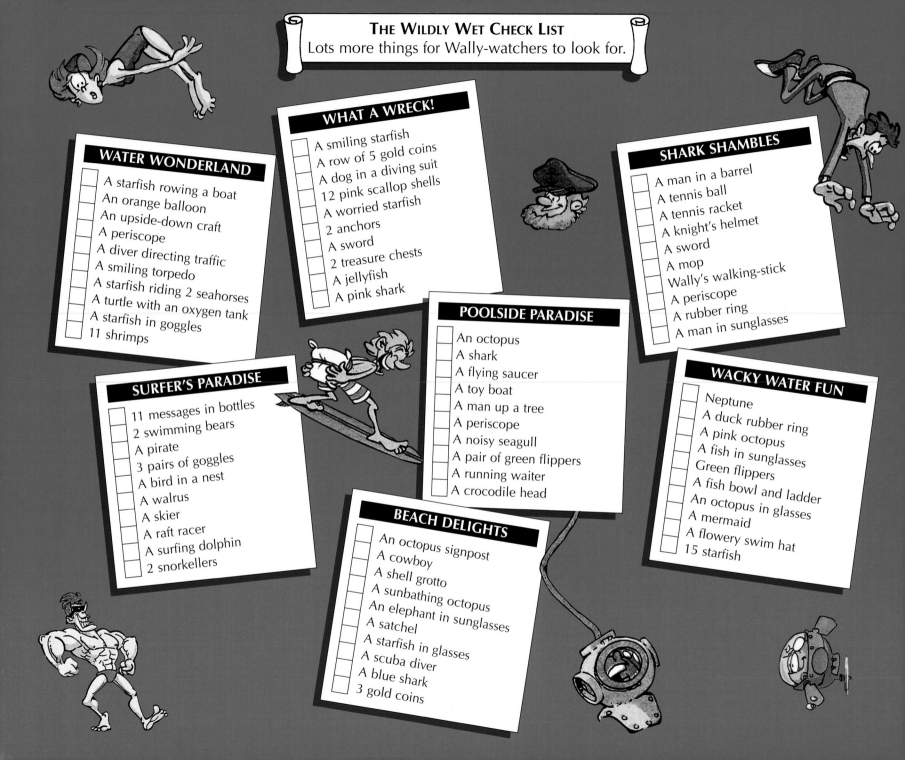

THE WILDLY WET CHECK LIST
Lots more things for Wally-watchers to look for.

WATER WONDERLAND
- A starfish rowing a boat
- An orange balloon
- An upside-down craft
- A periscope
- A diver directing traffic
- A smiling torpedo
- A starfish riding 2 seahorses
- A turtle with an oxygen tank
- A starfish in goggles
- 11 shrimps

WHAT A WRECK!
- A smiling starfish
- A row of 5 gold coins
- A dog in a diving suit
- 12 pink scallop shells
- A worried starfish
- 2 anchors
- A sword
- 2 treasure chests
- A jellyfish
- A pink shark

SHARK SHAMBLES
- A man in a barrel
- A tennis ball
- A tennis racket
- A knight's helmet
- A sword
- A mop
- Wally's walking-stick
- A periscope
- A rubber ring
- A man in sunglasses

SURFER'S PARADISE
- 11 messages in bottles
- 2 swimming bears
- A pirate
- 3 pairs of goggles
- A bird in a nest
- A walrus
- A skier
- A raft racer
- A surfing dolphin
- 2 snorkellers

POOLSIDE PARADISE
- An octopus
- A shark
- A flying saucer
- A toy boat
- A man up a tree
- A periscope
- A noisy seagull
- A pair of green flippers
- A running waiter
- A crocodile head

WACKY WATER FUN
- Neptune
- A duck rubber ring
- A pink octopus
- A fish in sunglasses
- Green flippers
- A fish bowl and ladder
- An octopus in glasses
- A mermaid
- A flowery swim hat
- 15 starfish

BEACH DELIGHTS
- An octopus signpost
- A cowboy
- A shell grotto
- A sunbathing octopus
- An elephant in sunglasses
- A satchel
- A starfish in glasses
- A scuba diver
- A blue shark
- 3 gold coins

Speech bubble text within illustration:

MOVE ALONG, FRIENDS,
FOR SOME MUSHROOM MAGIC. THEY
LIKE TO GROW IN DARK, DAMP PLACES
SO THIS CHAP IS BEING VERY USEFUL:
I'M WAY UP HIGH,
SMILING DOWN ON THEM ALL,
I TIP UP MY CAN
AND WATCH THE DROPS FALL.

HELP THIS
MUSHROOM FIND HIS CAP.

MUSHROOM MAGIC

DID YOU KNOW?

The stinkhorn fungus of Brazil can grow at the rate of 5 mm a minute. It reaches full size in 20 minutes.

Only 10 % of a mushroom appears above ground. The rest is a network of tiny strands winding through the ground.

Some forest fungi keep growing for hundreds of years and can end up weighing 100 tonnes – as much as a blue whale.

THINGS TO DO

Here are 5 pieces of picture. Three belong to this page and 2 come from somewhere else in the book. Can you find exactly where?

A
B
C
D
E

Which room can't you enter?

A mushroom.

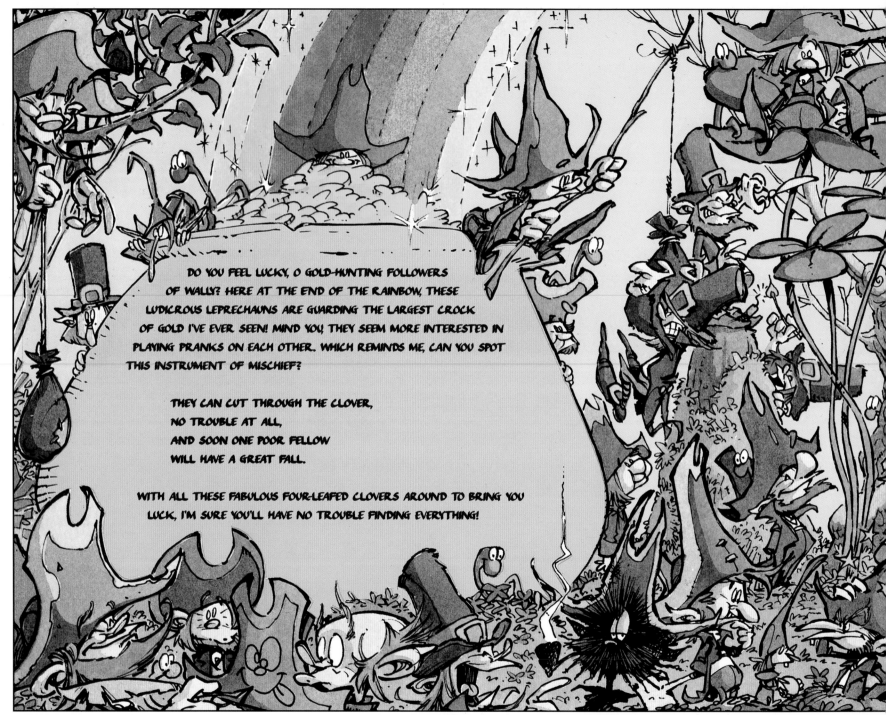

DO YOU FEEL LUCKY, O GOLD-HUNTING FOLLOWERS OF WALLY? HERE AT THE END OF THE RAINBOW, THESE LUDICROUS LEPRECHAUNS ARE GUARDING THE LARGEST CROCK OF GOLD I'VE EVER SEEN! MIND YOU, THEY SEEM MORE INTERESTED IN PLAYING PRANKS ON EACH OTHER. WHICH REMINDS ME, CAN YOU SPOT THIS INSTRUMENT OF MISCHIEF?

THEY CAN CUT THROUGH THE CLOVER,
NO TROUBLE AT ALL,
AND SOON ONE POOR FELLOW
WILL HAVE A GREAT FALL.

WITH ALL THESE FABULOUS FOUR-LEAFED CLOVERS AROUND TO BRING YOU LUCK, I'M SURE YOU'LL HAVE NO TROUBLE FINDING EVERYTHING!

HELP JIM THE LEPRECHAUN FIND HIS WAY TO THE COIN BEFORE HIS FRIENDS BEAT HIM TO IT.

LUDICROUS LEPRECHAUNS

DID YOU KNOW?

In Irish folklore, a leprechaun is a fairy who looks like a tiny old man, wearing a cocked hat and leather apron. Leprechauns are nearly always found making a single shoe.

If you capture a leprechaun you can force him to reveal his crock of gold, as long as you don't take your eyes off him.
He will try to trick you into looking away, and if you do he will vanish.

A four-leafed clover is not only lucky, it also protects the finder from fairy magic.

THINGS TO DO

The Leprechaun's Coin Trick

You need 3 coins, a pencil and some paper. Draw a straight line down the middle of the paper. Now, can you place the coins so that there are 2 heads on one side of the line and 2 tails on the other side? It's easier than you think!

What bow can't be tied?

A rainbow.

THESE POOR KNIGHTS HAVE GOT LOST IN THE WOODS AND ARE NOW IN A SPOT OF TROUBLE, O FAITHFUL FOLLOWERS OF WALLY. THIS ONE HAS CERTAINLY GOT MORE THAN HE BARGAINED FOR:

I'M CAUGHT IN A TRAP
AND BOUND IN GREEN ROPE.
FOR A CHANCE OF ESCAPE
I HAVEN'T A HOPE.

ONLY 2 OF THESE HELMETS ARE IDENTICAL. CAN YOU FIND WHICH ONES?

FOREST FUN

DID YOU KNOW?

Some trees can communicate with each other. If hungry caterpillars attack one, it will produce a chemical which makes it impossible for the caterpillars to digest. Other trees nearby, which are not even touching the attacked tree, sense the chemical in the air and start producing it too.

THINGS TO DO

The leader of the knights has sent an urgent message to his troops in hidden vowel-code. Can you decipher it using this key?

A	E	I	O	U
X	Y	Z	K	J

Z'VY HXD YNKJGH! LYT'S GYT KJT KF HYRY!

Now decipher this code to learn which knight is the leader.

HY HXS X GKLD HYLMYT WZTH XN KRXNGY FYXTHYR.

What makes a tree noisy?

Its bark.

DRAGON RIDE

DID YOU KNOW?

Dragons are entirely mythical creatures but they appear in the ancient cultures of many countries throughout the world.

The legends about dragons developed long before man had any knowledge of prehistoric animals.

Our word "dragon" comes from the Greek word *drakon*, which was used to describe any large serpent.

THINGS TO DO

Can you fill in the grid of mythical beasts using the central word and clues to help you?

1. Snake-headed woman
2. Half woman half fish
3. Half man half goat
4. Flying horse
5. White horse with one long horn
6. Half man half bull

		D	S	A	
		R	M		D
		S	A	T	
	P		G	S	
N	I		O		
M		N		T	

What kind of plane does a dragon fly?

A Spitfire.

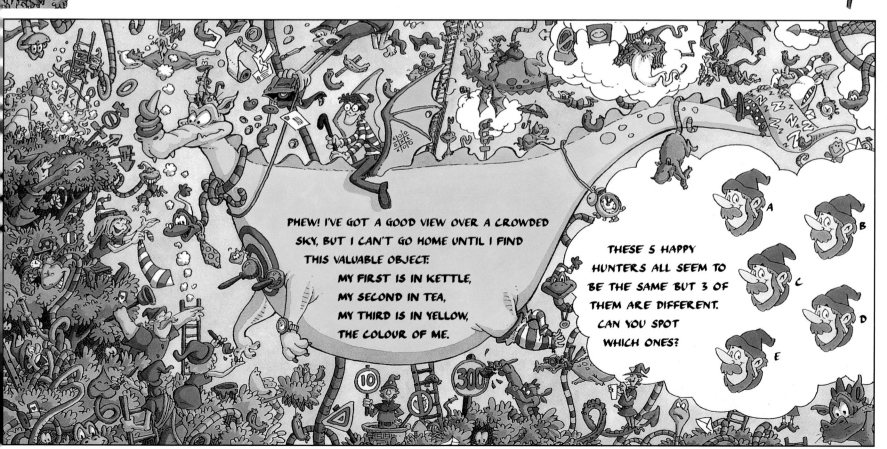

WELL, WALLY-WATCHERS, LOOK AT THIS MUSHROOM-MINING MADNESS.
I'M KEEPING WELL OUT OF THE WAY OF THESE CRAZY TROLLS, WHO DON'T
SEEM TO BE TOO ORGANIZED – AND SOME OF THOSE MUSHROOMS HAVE
MINDS OF THEIR OWN. THE TROLLS ARE SO BUSY THEY HAVEN'T NOTICED
SOMEONE SNEAKING AROUND, LOOKING FOR THE PRIZED GREEN
MUSHROOMS WITH RED SPOTS. CAN YOU SEE HIM? HERE'S A CLUE:

HE'S SITTING UP HIGH
IN A HAT AND A MASK,
TO STEAL PRECIOUS MUSHROOMS
IS HIS EVIL TASK.

HE LOOKS AS IF HE'S ALREADY GOT ONE UNSUSPECTING VICTIM.

MUSHROOM-MINING TROLLS

CAN YOU FIND A VICIOUS RED MUSHROOM, A RED AND ORANGE STRIPED MUSHROOM AND 9 RARE GREEN MUSHROOMS WITH RED SPOTS LIKE THE ONE BELOW?

WHEN YOU'VE FOUND ALL THESE TRY SAYING THIS TONGUETWISTER REALLY FAST WHILE WORKING OUT THE QUICKEST ROUTE TO THE MUSHROOM IN THE MIDDLE OF THE MAZE.

MRS MISSION MASHING MUSHROOMS

DID YOU KNOW?

Mushrooms are a fungus, made up mostly of water.

There are more than 70 species of poisonous mushrooms – some of them are deadly!

The largest recorded tree fungus has a circumference of 409 cm.

THINGS TO DO

Here are 4 pieces of picture. 2 belong to this page and 2 come from somewhere else in the book. Can you find exactly where they come from?

A
B
C
D

How would you know you had a toadstool in your dustbin?

* əpᴉsuᴉ ɯ ооɹɥsnɯ əq ʇ,uplnoʍ əɹəɥꓕ*

BETTER WATCH OUT, CUPID'S ABOUT AND LOVE IS IN THE AIR. CAN YOU SPOT THESE 2 ANIMALS, FAMOUS FOR NOT GETTING ON? THEY ONCE HAD A RACE, IT'S A TALE FROM THE PAST ONE SLOW BUT SURE, THE OTHER QUITE FAST.

ONLY ONE OF THESE SIX PICTURES IS EXACTLY THE SAME AS IN THE ORIGINAL. CAN YOU FIND IT?

CUPID CHAOS

DID YOU KNOW?

Cupid was the Roman god of love. He was often drawn as a child with wings, carrying a bow and arrow. Whoever he hit was destined to fall in love, but Cupid was blind and often made mistakes!

St Valentine's Day is on 14th February. It is the day when lovers send each other messages, often written in code or disguised handwriting to keep the loved one guessing. It is thought that Valentine's cards were the first greetings cards ever sent.

THINGS TO DO

Can you crack this saying, written in code. The clue is in every other letter:

ERLOENPDHGALNSTTSI
NBEOVTERRY
FXOFRHGNELT

Why did the cockerel fall in love with the hen?

She egged him on.

56

GREEN FOREST GAMES

DID YOU KNOW?

The first trees grew on Earth 280 million years ago.

The fastest growing tree in the world is the Eucalyptus. It can grow 3 cm in a day.

The slowest growing tree is the Sitka Spruce in the Arctic Circle. It can take 98 years to grow 28 cm.

THINGS TO DO

Grow your own trees.

Fill some small flower pots with potting compost and stand the pots in saucers. Collect pips from an orange, lemon or grapefruit and push them into the soil about 1 cm down – 1 pip per pot. Keep them in a warm, light place and water them frequently. As the seedlings get bigger, you may have to put them in bigger pots. You will never have fruit, but they look pretty and sometimes the leaves smell strongly.

What tree do hands grow on?   A palm tree.

EMERALDA AND THE GREEN FOREST WOMEN HAVE JOINED FORCES WITH THE MUDMEN TO RECLAIM THEIR TREE FROM THE BUCKET-HEAD KNIGHTS, AND THERE'S NO MESSING WITH THAT COMBINATION. THE WHOLE OF THE FOREST SEEMS TO BE ON THEIR SIDE. CAN YOU FIND THIS NOISY ANIMAL?

MY FEATHERS ARE RUFFLED
BY THESE BUCKET-HEAD KNIGHTS
SO I SHOUT AT THEM, "QUACK"
AND GIVE THEM A FRIGHT.
HIS BUCKET OPPONENT IS NOT AMUSED AND LOOKS
SET TO PLUNGE TO THE GROUND.
TIMBER!

THE NAMES OF 10 FAMILIAR TREES HAVE BEEN SPLIT UP. CAN YOU PUT THE CORRECT BITS TOGETHER AND FIND THE WORD FOR A TREE MUSEUM?

CED   UCE   ECH
  SYC   SPR
    AMORE   PLAR   WOOD
OA
      Y   WIL   AR   EW
TNUT
      PO   BE   K   ETUM
LOW
  ARBOR   RED   CHES

FOREST FUN

- A mud man in a helmet
- 2 stones tied to arrows
- A tree with a hole
- A yellow knight upside-down
- A stunned mud man
- 2 dogs with stripy tails
- A forest woman with a shield
- 2 stripy knights
- A large blue helmet
- 3 red plumes

MUSHROOM MAGIC

- A shouting mushroom
- A cheese-headed mushroom
- 2 umbrella caps
- A red bow
- 3 floating mushrooms
- A mushroom in sunglasses
- 5 stripy cap mushrooms
- A mushroom on a broomstick
- 9 tiny red cap mushrooms
- An axe

CUPID CHAOS

- 2 ladybirds
- A snail
- 12 red hearts
- A unicorn
- A yellow and blue butterfly
- A mouse
- A pink rabbit
- A fox
- 10 Cupids
- A yellow duck

DRAGON RIDE

- A magnifying glass
- A watch
- 3 mice
- A periscope
- 7 envelopes
- 3 clocks
- 2 fireman's hosepipes
- 2 playing cards
- Traffic lights
- 6 arrows

LUDICROUS LEPRECHAUNS

- A stick of dynamite
- A mallet
- A hat with a face
- A fishing rod
- A smouldering pipe
- 3 brown sacks of gold
- A feather pen
- 5 small gold hat buckles
- A bird's nest
- 13 snakes

GREEN FOREST GAMES

- A plant in a pot
- 2 woodpeckers
- A key
- 2 men on stilts
- A Tarzan dog
- 2 boxing gloves
- A worm
- A pair of shears
- 3 playing cards
- A spider

MUSHROOM-MINING TROLLS

- A walking-stick
- 2 red bottles
- 2 pairs of glasses
- A rake
- 2 periscopes
- A bossy green mushroom
- 3 blue forks
- A reading troll
- A tin can
- A pair of binoculars

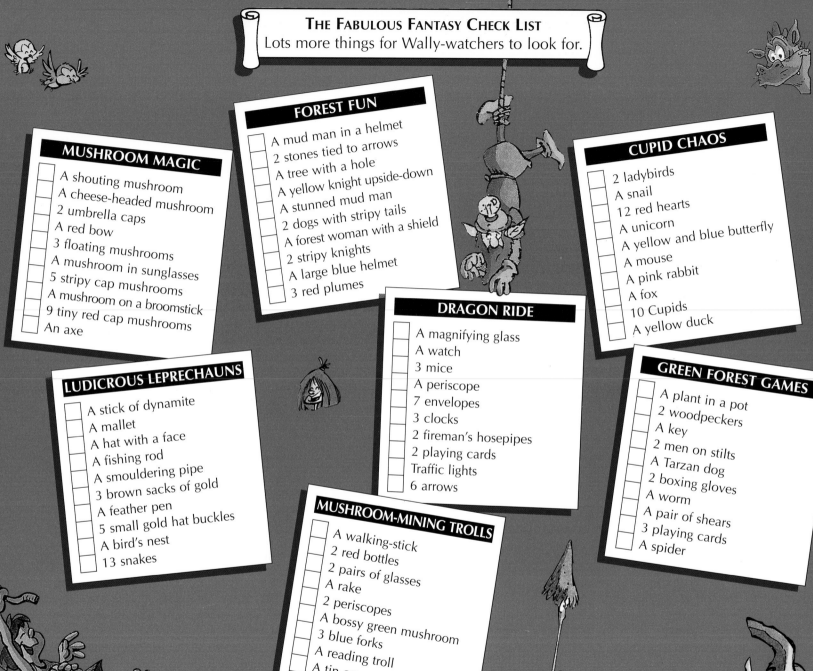

CAVE RAVE

DID YOU KNOW?

Neanderthal Man lived between 35,000 and 100,000 years ago. Fossil remains were found near the River Neander in Germany.

Although mammoths are now extinct we know a great deal about them as they were well preserved in the frozen ground of Northern Europe. Most mammoths were as big as elephants and were covered in long, shaggy hair.

THINGS TO DO

Try saying this tongue-twister as fast as you can:

Micky Mammoth met a massive monkey.
Did Micky Mammoth meet a massive monkey?
If Micky Mammoth met a massive monkey
Where's the massive monkey Micky met?

Is it hard to bury a dead mammoth?

Yes, it's a huge undertaking.

MEDIEVAL MAYHEM

DID YOU KNOW?

Some medieval castles have murder-holes through which sharp or heavy objects could be dropped from a great height on to enemies below.

Many castles have spiral staircases. Next time you visit an ancient castle notice how they always spiral up clockwise – the central pillar stopped anyone going up being able to brandish a sword properly.

THINGS TO DO

Can you find these 6 medieval words on the grid?

Turret	T O L S E M P
Spear	U S O H C O G
Moat	R O P I K A B
Shield	R U N E R T L
Keep	E U E L A S R
Tunic	T P H D I R D

What's the definition of attack?

A small nail.

WOW! THIS MEDIEVAL MAYHEM IS ENOUGH TO DRIVE ANYONE UP THE WALL. CAN YOU FIND ME IN THIS KNIGHT-TIME CHAOS, AND WHAT ABOUT THIS WEAPON THAT REALLY BELONGS IN THE KITCHEN? IT FLATTENS THE PASTRY, IT'S YELLOW AND ROUND, IT COULD KNOCK YOU OUT AS IT FALLS TO THE GROUND.

ALL BUT ONE OF THESE LITTLE PICTURES CAN BE FOUND IN THE MAIN SCENE. CAN YOU SPOT WHICH IS THE ODD ONE OUT?

A   B

C   D

E

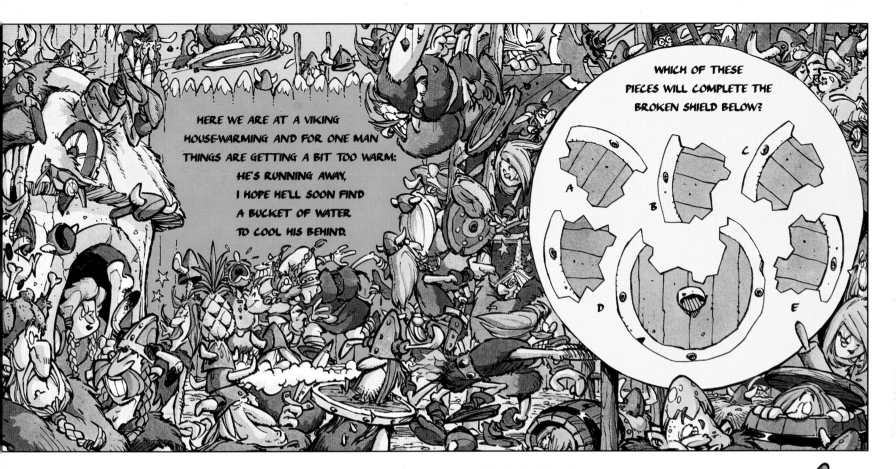

WHICH OF THESE PIECES WILL COMPLETE THE BROKEN SHIELD BELOW?

HERE WE ARE AT A VIKING HOUSE-WARMING AND FOR ONE MAN THINGS ARE GETTING A BIT TOO WARM: HE'S RUNNING AWAY, I HOPE HE'LL SOON FIND A BUCKET OF WATER TO COOL HIS BEHIND.

A B C D E

VIKING PARTY

DID YOU KNOW?

The Vikings believed in a giant sea serpent which stretched right round the world, gripping its tail in its mouth.

Unlike the Vikings in the picture, real Vikings did not wear horns in their helmets.

The longest Viking longboat ever was called "The Long Serpent". It was 37 m long and held over 60 oarsmen.

THINGS TO DO

Here are 4 pieces of picture. Two belong to this page and 2 come from somewhere else in the book. Can you find exactly where?

A   B   C   D

Where's the best place to hold a ship-board party?

Where the funnel be.

61

PIRATES AHOY

DID YOU KNOW?

There have been pirates in history as far back as Greek and Roman times.

Pirates were often recruited from naval crews who were no longer needed for war.

Many sixteenth century galleons carried cannons which could shoot nearly 15 kg of shot.

THINGS TO DO

In the mayhem these pirates tore up a scroll containing clues to hidden treasure. Each clue was ripped in half. Can you put them back together? To find out where the treasure lies, take the first word of the first sentence, the second of the second and so on.

1 It's easy	the anchor.
2 Look in	to find.
3 Then weigh	crow's flying.
4 See how the	a gull's nest.
5 And find	the hold.

Why does the sea never fall over the horizon?   *It's tide.*

OH AAARGH, ME HEARTIES, THERE'S TROUBLE ON BOARD! LOOKS LIKE A BIT OF A MUTINY. THERE'S ONE LADY PIRATE ON BOARD HERE. CAN YOU FIND HER AND WORK OUT HER NAME? TAKE THE FIRST HALF OF FLOWER, THE FIRST LETTER OF RINGS, ADD AN "A" AT THE END AND SEE HOW SHE SWINGS.

CAN YOU FIND 2 IDENTICAL BONES WHICH HAVE FALLEN OFF THE FLAG?

WILD WEST HEROES

DID YOU KNOW?

The era of the cowboy was the nineteenth century when beef was a profitable business in America. A herd of 2,500 cattle was looked after by 8 to 12 cowboys. It was Hollywood that gave cowboys their tough image.

Rodeos are competitions in which cowboys show off their skills. One of the best known exhibitions is the bucking bronco when a rider tries to stay on an unbroken horse.

THINGS TO DO

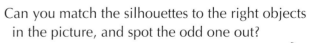

Can you match the silhouettes to the right objects in the picture, and spot the odd one out?

The odd shape out comes from another picture in the book; can you find which one?

Where do cowboys keep their water supply?
In their ten gallon hats.

I'M ON VACATION WITH THE VIKINGS AND
THEY CERTAINLY KNOW HOW TO ENJOY THEMSELVES.
WATER SPORTS SEEM TO BE THEIR SPECIALITY – I'LL TRY AND KEEP
OUT OF THE WAY TO AVOID GETTING WET.

ONE VIKING HAS NOT GIVEN HIMSELF THE DAY OFF, HOWEVER:

WHILE EVERYONE'S PLAYING
HE'S UP ON THE MAST.
HE'LL MAKE SURE THIS LONG BOAT
IS GLEAMING AT LAST.

CAN YOU SPOT WHICH VIKING HELMET BELOW IS THE ODD ONE OUT?

THE VIKINGS WERE GREAT
WARRIORS OF THE 9TH AND 11TH
CENTURIES, WHO RAIDED MANY COUNTRIES.
ON THIS GRID ARE THE NAMES OF 6 PLACES
THE VIKINGS INVADED. CAN YOU SPOT THEM ALL?

```
G P O I F U V S
R S B S R D O H
E N G L A N D E
E T R P N C D T
N O C O C A G L
L L H T E T E A
A M L F A L P N
N R U S S I A D
D N A L E R I S
```

THE VIKINGS

DID YOU KNOW?

The Vikings sometimes gave their swords names and passed them down through the generations.

Different classes of Viking society worshipped different gods. The chieftains looked to Odin, and the freemen and women to Thor. The slaves were thought too lowly to have a god.

Some Vikings were buried in graves which were outlined with stones set in a boat shape.

THINGS TO DO

Can you match the silhouettes to the correct part of the picture? 2 shapes come from other scenes in the book. Can you find which ones?

What did the Vikings use for secret messages? Norse code.

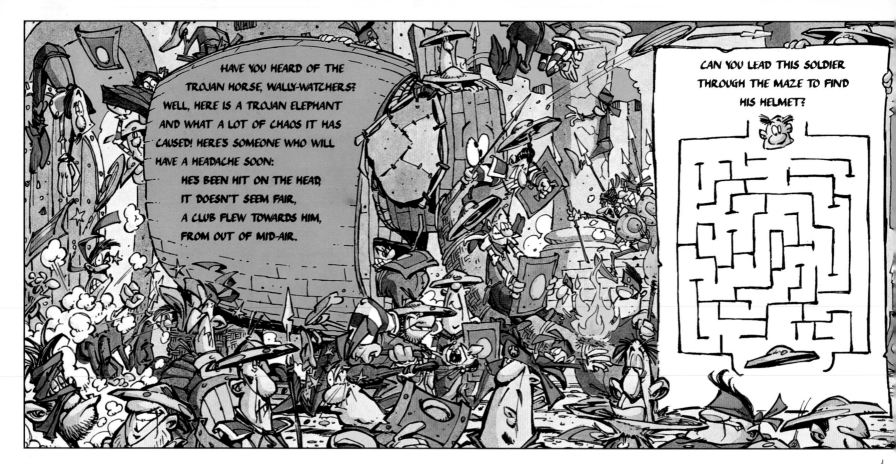

HAVE YOU HEARD OF THE TROJAN HORSE, WALLY-WATCHERS? WELL, HERE IS A TROJAN ELEPHANT AND WHAT A LOT OF CHAOS IT HAS CAUSED! HERE'S SOMEONE WHO WILL HAVE A HEADACHE SOON:

HE'S BEEN HIT ON THE HEAD,
IT DOESN'T SEEM FAIR,
A CLUB FLEW TOWARDS HIM,
FROM OUT OF MID-AIR.

CAN YOU LEAD THIS SOLDIER THROUGH THE MAZE TO FIND HIS HELMET?

TROJAN ELEPHANT

DID YOU KNOW?

The legend is that the Greeks besieged the city of Troy for 10 years. At last, the hero Odysseus had the idea of building a giant wooden horse and filling it with soldiers. It was left outside the gates and when the Trojans brought it in, the Greek soldiers crept out.

The Egyptian Pharaoh Psamtik I besieged the city of Azotus in Israel for 29 years in the 7th century BC. He could have done with a wooden horse!

THINGS TO DO

All these mixed up words can be found in the picture. Unjumble the letters to fill the grid, then read down the middle column to find out how I eventually escaped from the scene.

HLIEDS   PARES

RIFE

GEESI

SLAWL   DORIELS

What game do elephants play in a car?

ʎsɐnbs

ARMOURED KNIGHTS

DID YOU KNOW?

Chinese knights of the 11th century BC wore armour made from up to 7 layers of rhinoceros skin.

Some knights on the crusades died when their heads grew so hot inside their stifling armour that their brains boiled.

A suit of armour made for Archduke Maximilian II of Austria in 1548 had 123 separate pieces.

THINGS TO DO

When they're not fighting ferociously these naughty knights like testing tongue-twisters to keep their tonsils tight. How fast can you say these two?

Nine white knights tried tying twine.

My aching arm's armour's ancient.

Who wore the biggest boots in a medieval army?

The soldier with the biggest feet.

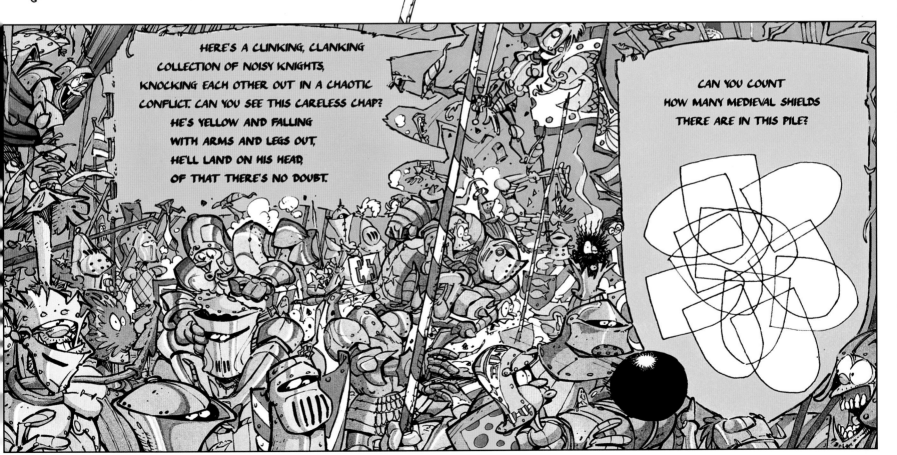

HERE'S A CLINKING, CLANKING COLLECTION OF NOISY KNIGHTS, KNOCKING EACH OTHER OUT IN A CHAOTIC CONFLICT. CAN YOU SEE THIS CARELESS CHAP? HE'S YELLOW AND FALLING WITH ARMS AND LEGS OUT, HE'LL LAND ON HIS HEAD, OF THAT THERE'S NO DOUBT.

CAN YOU COUNT HOW MANY MEDIEVAL SHIELDS THERE ARE IN THIS PILE?

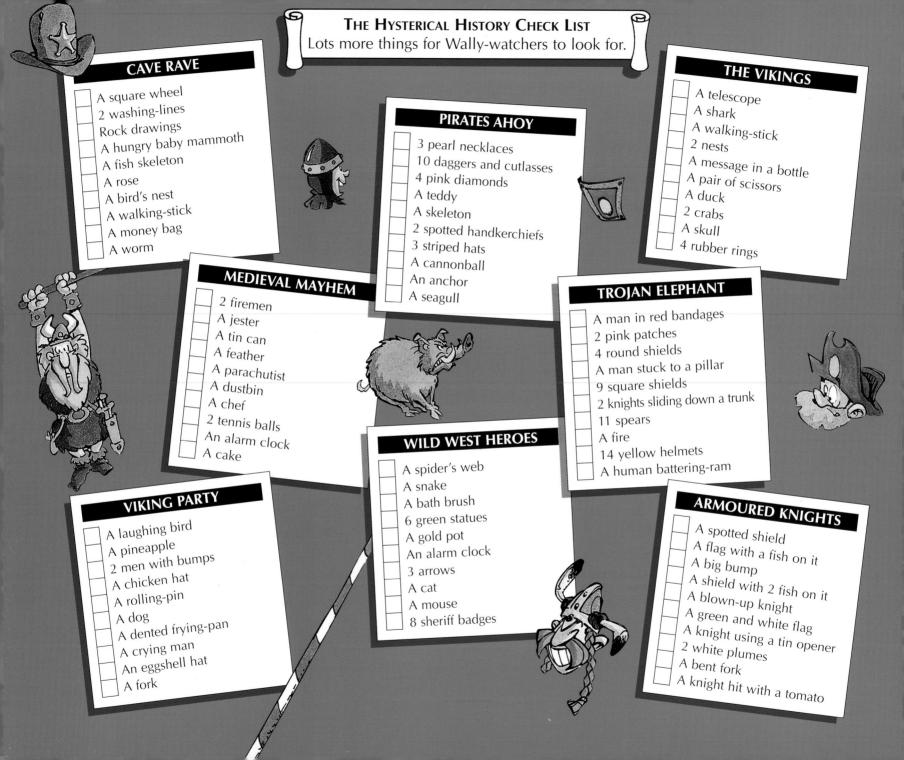

THE HYSTERICAL HISTORY CHECK LIST
Lots more things for Wally-watchers to look for.

CAVE RAVE
- A square wheel
- 2 washing-lines
- Rock drawings
- A hungry baby mammoth
- A fish skeleton
- A rose
- A bird's nest
- A walking-stick
- A money bag
- A worm

PIRATES AHOY
- 3 pearl necklaces
- 10 daggers and cutlasses
- 4 pink diamonds
- A teddy
- A skeleton
- 2 spotted handkerchiefs
- 3 striped hats
- A cannonball
- An anchor
- A seagull

THE VIKINGS
- A telescope
- A shark
- A walking-stick
- 2 nests
- A message in a bottle
- A pair of scissors
- A duck
- 2 crabs
- A skull
- 4 rubber rings

MEDIEVAL MAYHEM
- 2 firemen
- A jester
- A tin can
- A feather
- A parachutist
- A dustbin
- A chef
- 2 tennis balls
- An alarm clock
- A cake

TROJAN ELEPHANT
- A man in red bandages
- 2 pink patches
- 4 round shields
- A man stuck to a pillar
- 9 square shields
- 2 knights sliding down a trunk
- 11 spears
- A fire
- 14 yellow helmets
- A human battering-ram

WILD WEST HEROES
- A spider's web
- A snake
- A bath brush
- 6 green statues
- A gold pot
- An alarm clock
- 3 arrows
- A cat
- A mouse
- 8 sheriff badges

VIKING PARTY
- A laughing bird
- A pineapple
- 2 men with bumps
- A chicken hat
- A rolling-pin
- A dog
- A dented frying-pan
- A crying man
- An eggshell hat
- A fork

ARMOURED KNIGHTS
- A spotted shield
- A flag with a fish on it
- A big bump
- A shield with 2 fish on it
- A blown-up knight
- A green and white flag
- A knight using a tin opener
- 2 white plumes
- A bent fork
- A knight hit with a tomato

JUNGLE GYM

DID YOU KNOW?

Gorillas do not normally drink. They get all the moisture they need from the leaves, fruits and nuts they eat.

The Bee hummingbird is the world's smallest bird, measuring only 5 cm long, half of which is beak and tail.

Over half the world's 8,600 species of bird live in the Amazon rainforest.

THINGS TO DO

This word-snake has swallowed 6 jungle animals. Can you read the letters from right to left and work out which ones?

RIPATALUTNARATTNAERIFROTAGILLAGORFEERTAMUP

He won't need another meal for a while, will he?

Why is a monkey like a flower? Because it is a chimp-pansy.

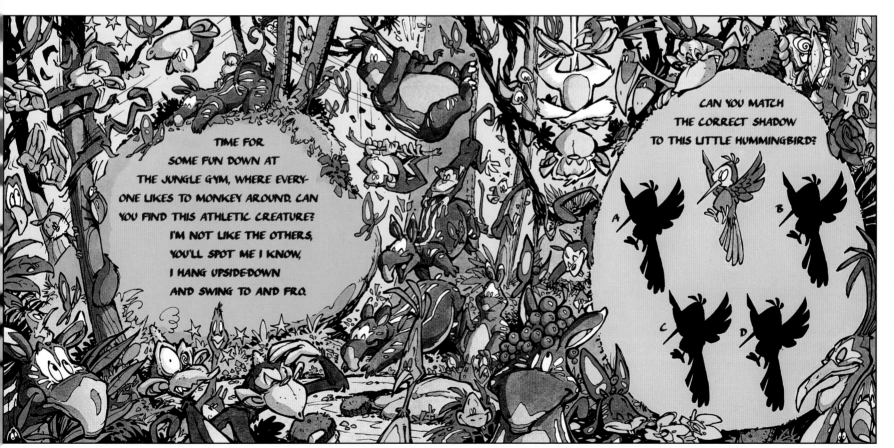

TIME FOR SOME FUN DOWN AT THE JUNGLE GYM, WHERE EVERYONE LIKES TO MONKEY AROUND. CAN YOU FIND THIS ATHLETIC CREATURE? I'M NOT LIKE THE OTHERS, YOU'LL SPOT ME I KNOW, I HANG UPSIDEDOWN AND SWING TO AND FRO.

CAN YOU MATCH THE CORRECT SHADOW TO THIS LITTLE HUMMINGBIRD?

A B C D

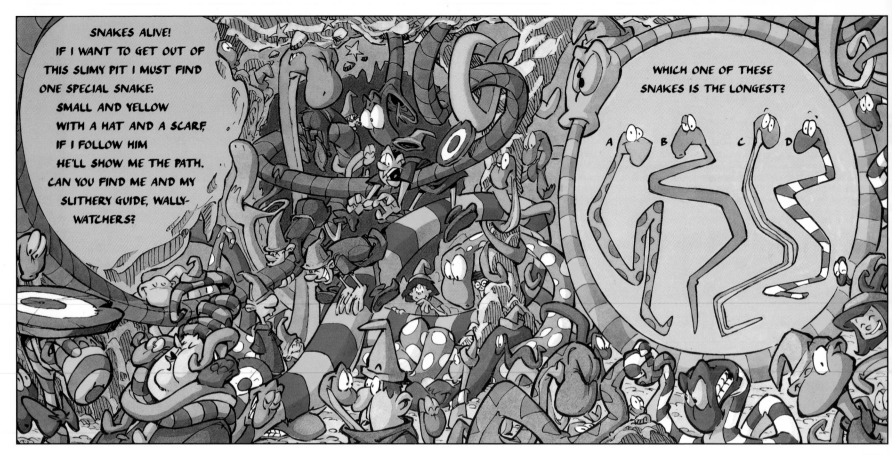

SNAKE PIT

DID YOU KNOW?

One of the biggest snakes ever found was an Anaconda. It was 8.45 metres long with a girth of 111 centimetres.

Most pythons kill their prey by constricting or squeezing it, and the larger species can swallow animals as big as goats and pigs.

Snakes grow continuously throughout their lives, shedding their skins when they outgrow them.

THINGS TO DO

How many different snakes can you read here?

Why can you never play a trick on a snake?
Because you can't pull its leg.

DINOSAUR GAMES

DID YOU KNOW?

Dinosaurs actually roamed the earth for 165 million years before they became extinct.

The largest dinosaur was the Brachiosaurus. It weighed about the same as 20 elephants.

In some places archaeologists have discovered 2 sets of dinosaur tracks next to each other which may mean that some dinosaurs used to walk side by side for company.

THINGS TO DO

How many different words can you make out of:

TYRANNOSAURUS REX

Rating: 20, good; 30, very good; more than 50, truly astonishing!

Try saying this tongue-twister as fast as you can:
Tiny Timmy Tyrannosaurus took the train to Transylvania.

Why did the dinosaur cross the road?
Because the chicken hadn't been invented.

AMAZING!
HAVE YOU EVER SEEN SUCH A COLLECTION OF DIPPY DINOS? I HAD NO IDEA THEY HAD SUCH FUN AND GAMES. TALKING OF GAMES, THERE'S SOMETHING IN THIS PICTURE THAT'S GOT LOST IN TIME. IT LOOKS LIKE AN EGG LAID IN A NEST, BUT IT'S YELLOW AND ROUND AND WON'T HATCH LIKE THE REST.

THIS DAFT DINO IS MADE OF BITS FROM 6 REAL DINOSAURS. CAN YOU RECOGNIZE ALL OF THEM?

WELL, HERE'S A BIT OF MONKEY BUSINESS. HE HAS JUST DROPPED IN TO SAY HALLO – BUT HE DOESN'T KNOW HIS OWN STRENGTH. CAN YOU SPOT THIS POOR MAN WHO LOOKS VERY CROSS AT BEING DISTURBED?
HE'S ON THE TOP FLOOR
AND LOOKS PRETTY MAD,
HE'S MISSING THE DINNER
HE THOUGHT HE ONCE HAD.
PHEW! THIS WAS AN EARTH-SHATTERING EXPERIENCE.

WHICH SILHOUETTE EXACTLY MATCHES THE FEARLESS FLIER BELOW?

A B
C D

MONKEY MISCHIEF

DID YOU KNOW?

Monkeys and apes are different. A monkey has a long tail and an ape has such a short tail it cannot be seen.

The tallest gorilla measured 1.88 m high.

The smallest known monkey is the Pygmy Marmoset, which is about 14 cm long.

THINGS TO DO

In the letter maze below there are 10 animals – 5 across and 5 down. Pick either letter from each pair and find a hidden animal, reading across each line once. Then take the leftover letters and read the animals down.

H T	C I	P G	E S	R H
M O	O H	A U	H S	E Y
R Z	E I	N B	R E	A E
S C	A M	D M	E E	L N
W E	H P	A A	P L	A E

How does a monkey cook his toast?

On a gorilla.

72

DEEP SEA DIVING

DID YOU KNOW?

All sorts of weird and wonderful creatures live on the bottom of the deep sea bed. It's so dark down there that some fish make themselves glow with light to attract prey, confuse an enemy or find a mate.

The octopus is thought to be the most intelligent of all invertebrates. When in danger it squirts out ink to make a screen to hide behind.

THINGS TO DO

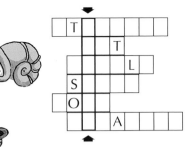

TEN

OKOH   RUTSEARE

RITSHAFS   SRCLOL

LSELH

Sort out the jumbled letters and fit them into the grid. What is the very useful seafaring word in the middle?

How does an octopus go into battle?

Well armed.

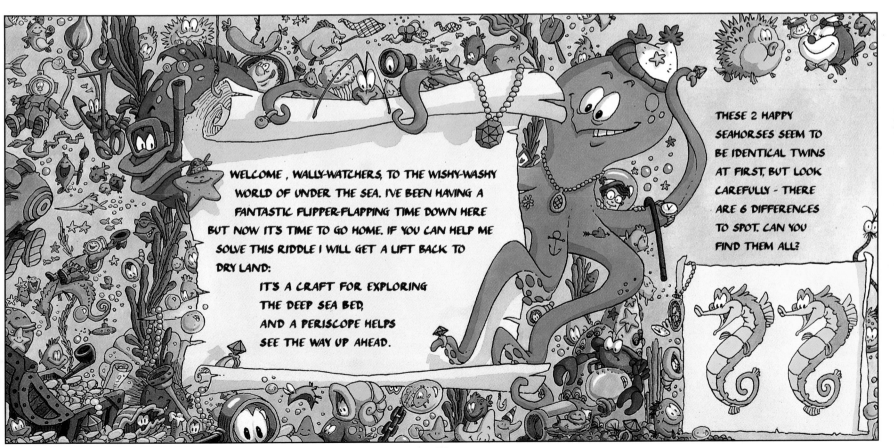

WELCOME, WALLY-WATCHERS, TO THE WISHY-WASHY WORLD OF UNDER THE SEA. I'VE BEEN HAVING A FANTASTIC FLIPPER-FLAPPING TIME DOWN HERE BUT NOW IT'S TIME TO GO HOME. IF YOU CAN HELP ME SOLVE THIS RIDDLE I WILL GET A LIFT BACK TO DRY LAND:

IT'S A CRAFT FOR EXPLORING THE DEEP SEA BED, AND A PERISCOPE HELPS SEE THE WAY UP AHEAD.

THESE 2 HAPPY SEAHORSES SEEM TO BE IDENTICAL TWINS AT FIRST, BUT LOOK CAREFULLY - THERE ARE 6 DIFFERENCES TO SPOT. CAN YOU FIND THEM ALL?

JURASSIC HIGH-JINKS

DID YOU KNOW?

An Allosaurus could have eaten a human being in 2 mouthfuls.

Some dinosaurs could run at the speed of 65 km/h which would have outrun an ostrich.

A Stegosaurus had a body as long as a bus, but a brain the size of a walnut.

THINGS TO DO

Pterodactyl Crunch: A game for 2 players. You will need paper, scissors and a chair.

Cut the paper into 20 Pterodactyl shapes. One player is the Tyrannosaur, the other stands on the chair and drops the Pterodactyls, one by one. The Tyrannosaur must catch each Pterodactyl between first finger and thumb, before it hits the ground. When all 20 have been dropped, swap over.

The winner is the Tyrannosaur who catches the most Pterodactyls for lunch.

How do dinosaurs pass exams?

With extinction.

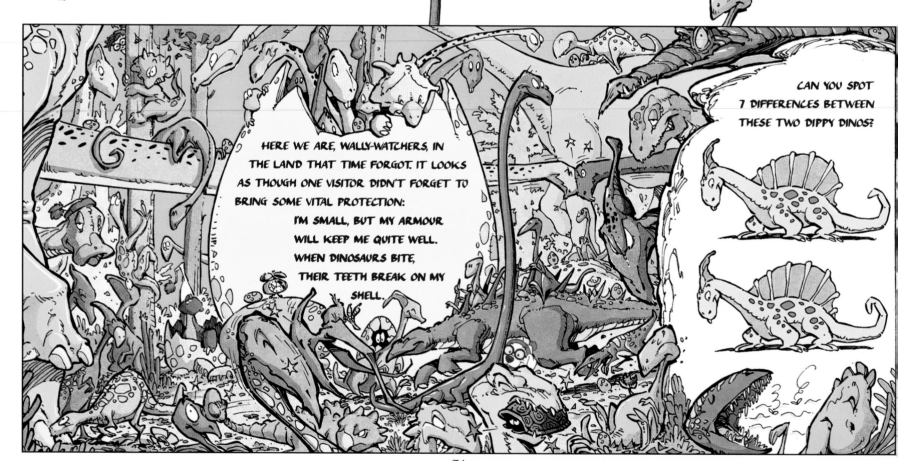

HERE WE ARE, WALLY-WATCHERS, IN THE LAND THAT TIME FORGOT. IT LOOKS AS THOUGH ONE VISITOR DIDN'T FORGET TO BRING SOME VITAL PROTECTION:

I'M SMALL, BUT MY ARMOUR WILL KEEP ME QUITE WELL. WHEN DINOSAURS BITE, THEIR TEETH BREAK ON MY SHELL.

CAN YOU SPOT 7 DIFFERENCES BETWEEN THESE TWO DIPPY DINOS?

DOG DAYS

DID YOU KNOW?

A dog called Braeburns's Close Encounter held the record for the most "Best in Show" awards. He won 203.

The biggest litter of any dog was 23 puppies, born to an American fox-hound called Lena.

There are over 400 species of dog in the world.

THINGS TO DO

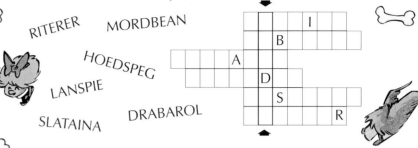

Unjumble the dog breeds below and fit them into the grid to find out who eventually won the show.

RITERER   MORDBEAN

HOEDSPEG

LANSPIE

SLATAINA   DRABAROL

What did the dog say when he sat on a piece of sandpaper? ¡ɟɟnᴚ

PHEW! THIS CHAOS SHOULD GIVE YOU PAWS FOR THOUGHT. I WOULDN'T WANT TO JUDGE THIS COMPETITION, ANYWAY IT MIGHT BE A LITTLE DIFFICULT NOW. THE COVER IS GREEN IT'S UP IN THE AIR IT'S FULL OF THE RULES TO MAKE SURE THE SHOW'S FAIR. TIME FOR ME TO TAKE MY BOW.

CAN YOU TELL WHERE THESE 4 PICTURES COME FROM IN THIS SCENE?

THEY SAY BIRDS OF A FEATHER STICK TOGETHER AND THAT'S CERTAINLY TRUE OF THIS BUNCH OF FOOLISH FOWL. I'VE GOT A BIRD'S EYE VIEW, WALLY-WATCHERS. CAN YOU SPOT ME AMONG ALL THESE CRASH LANDINGS? AND WHERE IS THIS SMART FELLOW? HE'S SURELY HIGH UP IN THE PECKING ORDER: I'M BLACK AND WHITE WITH A PINK BOW TIE, MY LEGS ARE SO LONG I CAN HARDLY FLY.

HERE'S AN EGGSTRAORDINARY PUZZLE. CAN YOU WORK OUT WHICH PIECE BELOW COMPLETES THE BROKEN EGG?

BIRD BRAINS

DID YOU KNOW?

A bird's bones are almost hollow so that they are very light. Often a bird's skeleton weighs less than its feathers.

Swifts spend 2 to 3 years at a time in the air, never setting foot on land. They even sleep on the wing!

There is a budgerigar in the USA that has a talking vocabulary of 1,728 words!

THINGS TO DO

Here are 7 bird circle puzzles. To solve each one start at any corner and read clockwise or anticlockwise.

Which bird is always out of breath?

A puffin.

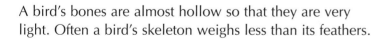

SNAKY GAMES

DID YOU KNOW?

After eating a large animal, a python may not need to eat again for over a month.

One boa constrictor is known to have lived for over 40 years.

Pit vipers have heat sensitive cells in their heads and they can sense the warmth of a small animal's body several metres away in the dark.

THINGS TO DO

Here are 3 slippery snake tongue-twisters. Say them as fast as you can without tying your tongue in knots!

My sister constrictor constricts a constructor.

Five vile vipers filing.

I saw seven saucy snakes slither sideways.

What happened to the snake with a cold?   *She had to viper nose.*

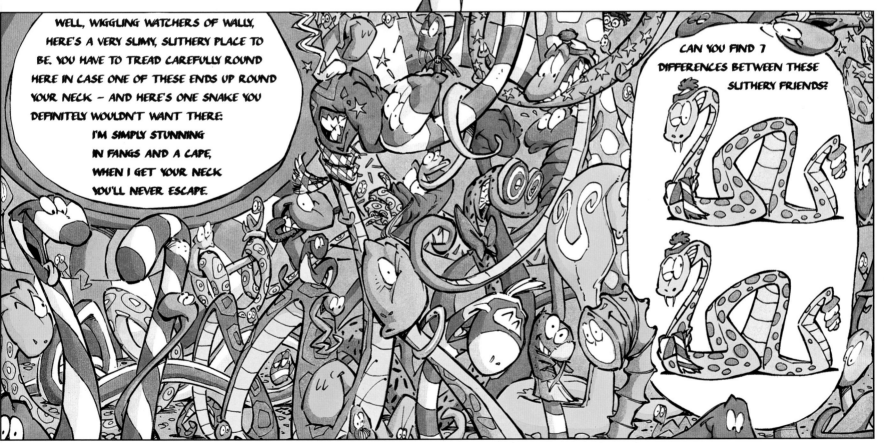

WELL, WIGGLING WATCHERS OF WALLY, HERE'S A VERY SLIMY, SLITHERY PLACE TO BE. YOU HAVE TO TREAD CAREFULLY ROUND HERE IN CASE ONE OF THESE ENDS UP ROUND YOUR NECK – AND HERE'S ONE SNAKE YOU DEFINITELY WOULDN'T WANT THERE. I'M SIMPLY STUNNING IN FANGS AND A CAPE, WHEN I GET YOUR NECK YOU'LL NEVER ESCAPE.

CAN YOU FIND 7 DIFFERENCES BETWEEN THESE SLITHERY FRIENDS?

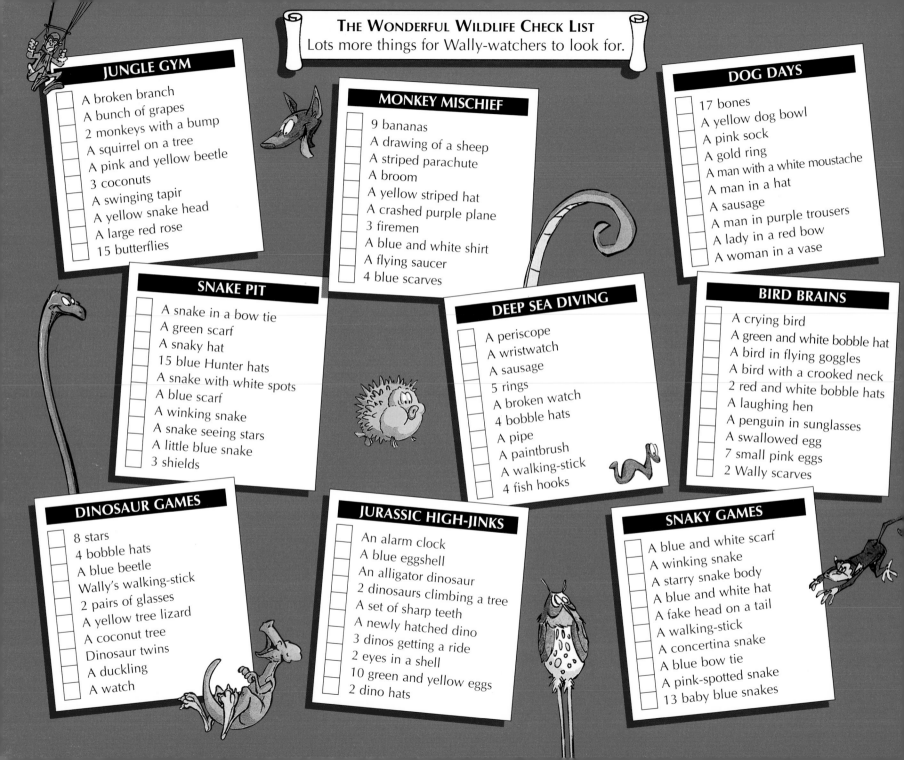

THE WONDERFUL WILDLIFE CHECK LIST
Lots more things for Wally-watchers to look for.

JUNGLE GYM
- A broken branch
- A bunch of grapes
- 2 monkeys with a bump
- A squirrel on a tree
- A pink and yellow beetle
- 3 coconuts
- A swinging tapir
- A yellow snake head
- A large red rose
- 15 butterflies

MONKEY MISCHIEF
- 9 bananas
- A drawing of a sheep
- A striped parachute
- A broom
- A yellow striped hat
- A crashed purple plane
- 3 firemen
- A blue and white shirt
- A flying saucer
- 4 blue scarves

DOG DAYS
- 17 bones
- A yellow dog bowl
- A pink sock
- A gold ring
- A man with a white moustache
- A man in a hat
- A sausage
- A man in purple trousers
- A lady in a red bow
- A woman in a vase

SNAKE PIT
- A snake in a bow tie
- A green scarf
- A snaky hat
- 15 blue Hunter hats
- A snake with white spots
- A blue scarf
- A winking snake
- A snake seeing stars
- A little blue snake
- 3 shields

DEEP SEA DIVING
- A periscope
- A wristwatch
- A sausage
- 5 rings
- A broken watch
- 4 bobble hats
- A pipe
- A paintbrush
- A walking-stick
- 4 fish hooks

BIRD BRAINS
- A crying bird
- A green and white bobble hat
- A bird in flying goggles
- A bird with a crooked neck
- 2 red and white bobble hats
- A laughing hen
- A penguin in sunglasses
- A swallowed egg
- 7 small pink eggs
- 2 Wally scarves

DINOSAUR GAMES
- 8 stars
- 4 bobble hats
- A blue beetle
- Wally's walking-stick
- 2 pairs of glasses
- A yellow tree lizard
- A coconut tree
- Dinosaur twins
- A duckling
- A watch

JURASSIC HIGH-JINKS
- An alarm clock
- A blue eggshell
- An alligator dinosaur
- 2 dinosaurs climbing a tree
- A set of sharp teeth
- A newly hatched dino
- 3 dinos getting a ride
- 2 eyes in a shell
- 10 green and yellow eggs
- 2 dino hats

SNAKY GAMES
- A blue and white scarf
- A winking snake
- A starry snake body
- A blue and white hat
- A fake head on a tail
- A walking-stick
- A concertina snake
- A blue bow tie
- A pink-spotted snake
- 13 baby blue snakes

SNOW SCULPTING

DID YOU KNOW?

No two snowflakes are exactly the same.

About $\frac{1}{10}$ of the Earth is permanently covered by ice, mostly in Antarctica and Greenland. If it all melted, the sea would rise by 60 m, drowning many large cities, including New York, London and Tokyo.

A glacier in Greenland moves as much as 19 m every day.

THINGS TO DO

Can you match the silhouettes to their originals?
Only 3 come from this page; the others can be found somewhere else in the book – can you find where?

What do you sing on a snowman's birthday?

"Freeze a jolly good fellow."

WOW! IT LOOKS AS THOUGH THESE STRANGE SNOWMEN ARE A LITTLE BORED WITH THEIR NORMAL SHAPES AND ARE EXPERIMENTING WITH NEW DESIGNS! AND CAN YOU SPOT THIS CLUMSY FELLOW? HE'S LEARNING TO JUGGLE, THERE'S A LONG WAY TO GO, ON HIS HEAD SOME SQUASHED FRUIT HAS COVERED THE SNOW.

WHICH 2 OF THESE THINGS DO NOT APPEAR IN THE PICTURE?

CAN YOU FIND 7 OF THESE
OBJECTS IN THE SHOPPING CENTRE?
WHICH 2 ARE MISSING?

SHOPPING HORROR

DID YOU KNOW?

 The world's largest shopping centre occupies the same amount of space as 58 football pitches.

Escalators rise at a maximum speed of 2.1 km/h.

THINGS TO DO

Wenda is off to the shops. She has to buy one thing in each of these places:

CLOTHES STORE, TOYSHOP, SPORTS SHOP, FOOD STORE.

 She must visit them in the order shown on the list. Unjumble the muddled words to work out what she had to buy where and which store is which. Then work out the route Wenda took, if she didn't retrace her steps once.

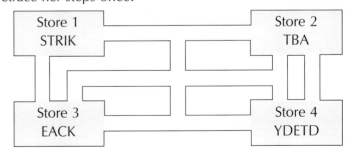

Store 1 STRIK	Store 2 TBA
Store 3 EACK	Store 4 YDETD

 When is a shop like a boat?

 When it has sales.

CRYSTAL CRATER

DID YOU KNOW?

The largest uncut diamond in the world was called the Cullinan. It weighed over ½ kg and was the size of a man's fist.

Rubies are rarer and more valuable than diamonds.

If all the gold mined since the Stone Age were gathered together, it would create a cube with a base the size of a tennis court!

THINGS TO DO

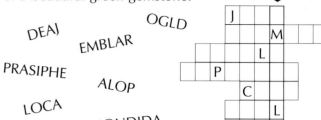

Here are 7 things people have mined. Unscramble the words and put them into the grid to get the name of a beautiful green gemstone.

DEAJ

EMBLAR

OGLD

PRASIPHE

ALOP

LOCA

MONDIDA

Where's the easiest place to find diamonds?   In a pack of cards.

WELL, MY SPARKLY-EYED FOLLOWERS, HAVE YOU EVER SEEN SO MANY PRECIOUS STONES ALL IN ONE PLACE! I'M SURE YOU'VE NEVER SEEN SUCH LIVELY ONES! I THINK SOMEONE HAS TAKEN A CHUNK OUT OF THIS ONE.
THERE ONCE WAS A DIAMOND
IN THE MIDDLE OF ME,
BUT NOW THERE'S A HOLE
WHERE MY MIDDLE SHOULD BE.

CAN YOU PUT THESE ROCKS INTO PAIRS AND FIND THE ODD ONE OUT?

CRAZY CARS

DID YOU KNOW?

If you could travel round the world in a car it would take you 453 hours, travelling at 55 mph. That's over 2^{1}/2 weeks.

In 1930 Charles Creighton and James Hargis drove their car all the way from New York to Los Angeles in reverse without stopping. They then drove all the way back in reverse. The whole trip took 42 days.

One of the longest traffic jams ever stretched 176 km between Lyon and Paris, France.

THINGS TO DO

How many words can you make out of

JUGGERNAUT

10, quite good; 20, good; over 30, simply sensational!

Why did the motorist drive her car in reverse?

Because she knew the rules of the road backwards.

SNOWSTORM

DID YOU KNOW?

Snowflakes are always hexagonal.
That means they always have 6 sides.

In September 1981 the temperature in the Kalahari Desert
in Africa dropped to 5°C and for the first
time in living memory there
was snow in
the desert.

The biggest snowman ever was over 19 metres high and took
a team 2 weeks to build. They called him Super Frosty.

THINGS TO DO

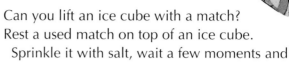

Can you lift an ice cube with a match?
Rest a used match on top of an ice cube.
Sprinkle it with salt, wait a few moments and
lift up the cube with
the match.
Easy!

How do you make anti-freeze?   *Hide her nightie.*

IT'S SNOW JOKE! THESE SNOWMEN
ARE COMPLETELY OUT OF CONTROL,
AND SOMEONE HAS BEEN PLAYING A
PRACTICAL JOKE ON ONE OF THEM.
CAN YOU SPOT WHO IT IS?
HE LOOKS MOST PECULIAR;
HE'LL NEED HELP WHEN HE'S FOUND.
ONE PART OF HIS BODY
IS THE WRONG WAY AROUND.

WHICH 3 PIECES FIT
TOGETHER TO MAKE THE
COMPLETE SNOW HEAD?

A

B

C

D

E

F

ALIEN INSECT SWAMP

DID YOU KNOW?

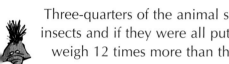

House flies can beat their wings 200 times per second and midges 1,000 times.

One acre of pasture-land contains about 360 million insects.

Three-quarters of the animal species in the world are insects and if they were all put together they would weigh 12 times more than the human population.

THINGS TO DO

Here are the names of 10 familiar insects which have been split up. Can you put the correct bits together and with the two pieces left over find the word for a beetle collector?

BUMBLE   AN   BEE   LADY   CRIC   MOS

KET   ERFLY   GRASS   T   BUTT

QUITO   COLEOP   LO   BIRD   TERIST   TLE

CUST   BEE   ITE   TERM   HOPPER

Where would you put an injured insect?   *·ǝɔuɐꞁnqɯɐ uɐ uꞀ*

SOMETHING'S BUGGING ME, WALLY-WATCHERS. IT MUST BE THE EFFECT OF HIDING IN THIS ALIEN INSECT SWAMP - FAR TOO MANY CREEPY CRAWLIES AND LONG-LEGGED BEASTIES FOR MY LIKING. PERHAPS IF I STAY HIDDEN I'LL BE SAFE AND WON'T SUFFER THE FATE OF THIS CHAP. CAN YOU SEE HIM?
HE CLINGS TO THE GRASS
WITH ALL HIS MIGHT,
A TONGUE HAS REACHED OUT
AND IS HOLDING HIM TIGHT.

CAN YOU MATCH THE CORRECT SHADOW TO THIS ALIEN BUG?

WOW! HOW ABOUT THIS FOR A FUN-FILLED FLIGHT OF FANCY? THIS IS THE BALLOON RACE OF A LIFETIME! I HOPE ALL THIS FLOATING AROUND DOESN'T MAKE YOU LIGHT-HEADED! UNBELIEVABLE! THERE GOES AN ALIEN IN A YELLOW ROCKET. CAN YOU SEE HIM TOO? AND WHAT ABOUT A MAGIC CARPET, A KNIGHT IN ARMOUR AND A MESSAGE IN A BOTTLE?

I SAW THE STRANGEST SIGHT OF ALL JUST NOW. HERE'S A CLUE TO HELP YOU SPOT WHAT IT WAS:

HE'S GREEN AND HE'S CROAKING;
BELIEVE ME, IT'S TRUE!
HE'S SITTING IN WATER,
ADMIRING THE VIEW!

BETTER CATCH HIM BEFORE HE GOES UP, UP AND AWAY. AS EACH BALLOON ENTERED THE RACE THEY WERE GIVEN A NUMBER. THE VERY LAST COMPETITOR, THE ONE WITH THE HIGHEST NUMBER APPEARS IN THIS PICTURE. CAN YOU FIND IT?

ONLY 5 OF THESE PICTURES
CAN BE FOUND IN OUR HOT AIR SCENE.
CAN YOU SPOT THE ODD ONE OUT?

WHEN YOU'VE FOUND THE ONE THAT
DOESN'T FIT, LOOK THROUGH THE REST OF THE
BOOK TO DISCOVER WHICH INCREDIBLE WALLY SCENE
IT BELONGS TO:

A   B   C

D   E   F

PHEW! I DON'T KNOW ABOUT YOU BUT
I'M GETTING CARRIED AWAY - THIS
IS SUCH AN UPLIFTING
EXPERIENCE! !

BALLOON RACE

DID YOU KNOW?

Joseph and Étienne Montgolfier launched a hot air balloon on 19th September 1783 which carried a sheep, a cockerel and a duck. It flew for 8 minutes.

On 21st November 1783 Francois Laurent and Jean François Pilâtre de Rozier were the first people to sail in a hot air balloon. They sailed over Paris for about 9 km and burned wool and straw to keep the air in the balloon hot.

Napoleon used hot air balloons as anchored observation points in some of his battles.

THINGS TO DO

Invincible balloon
Did you know that if you place a piece of sticky-tape over a blown-up balloon and then stick a pin through the tape, the balloon will not burst!
Try it yourself and see!

Water-bending balloon trick
Turn on a cold water tap. Rub a blown-up balloon on your sleeve and then hold it next to the running water (but don't let the balloon actually touch the water). See how the balloon static bends the water.

What did the balloon say to the pin?   ¡Hi buster!

TRAFFIC JAM

DID YOU KNOW?

In 1990 1½ million cars were caught in a traffic jam to cross the East-West German border when the Berlin Wall came down.

The first traffic signals were put up in Parliament Square in London, England, in 1868.

Traffic policemen in Tokyo have to wear smog-masks to protect them from pollution.

THINGS TO DO

Find your way from the bus to another form of transport by following the clues to each word and changing 1 letter each time. The first change has been made for you.

	BUS
"Tub" backwards	BUT
A small shack	_ _ _
Worn on the head	_ _ _
A feline friend	_ _ _
Your new vehicle	_ _ _

Why can't a car play football?   Because it's only got one boot.

OH DEAR! HERE'S A TRAFFIC JAM YOU WOULDN'T WANT TO GET STUCK IN EVERY DAY. THAT LITTLE GREEN CAR WITH EXTENDING LEGS SEEMS TO HAVE THE RIGHT IDEA AND HE'S GOT A GOOD VIEW. CAN YOU SPOT THIS UNIQUE LITTLE ANIMAL DRIVER?

HE'S DRIVING ALONG,
JUST HAVING A LAUGH,
IN GOGGLES, A HELMET
AND A FLUFFY PINK SCARF.

TWO OF THESE CARS ARE IDENTICAL. CAN YOU WORK OUT WHICH?

A B C D E F

WALLY LOOKALIKE

DID YOU KNOW?

Animals in forests and long grasslands are often striped to merge with the background.

Animals out in the open have spotted camouflage to hide among rocks and stones.

The chameleon cannot change colour to match its surroundings, but only in response to temperature, light, anger and fear.

THINGS TO DO

How many words can you find hidden inside:

CAMOUFLAGE

10, quite good;
20, very good;
over 30, improbably impressive!

Who went into the tiger's den and came out alive? *The tiger.*

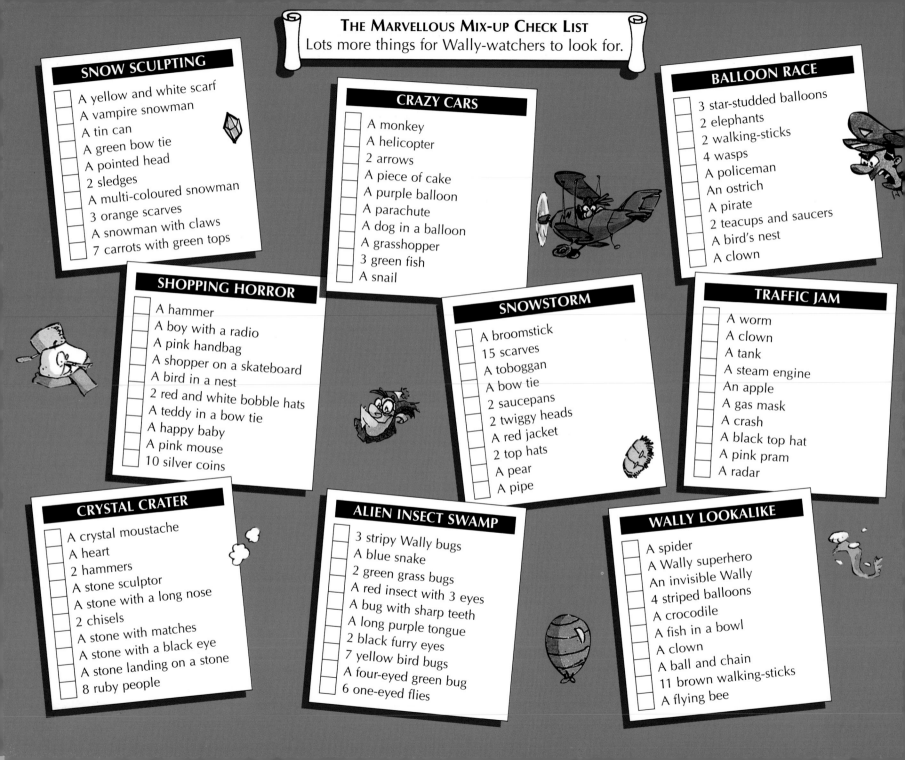

THE MARVELLOUS MIX-UP CHECK LIST
Lots more things for Wally-watchers to look for.

SNOW SCULPTING
- A yellow and white scarf
- A vampire snowman
- A tin can
- A green bow tie
- A pointed head
- 2 sledges
- A multi-coloured snowman
- 3 orange scarves
- A snowman with claws
- 7 carrots with green tops

CRAZY CARS
- A monkey
- A helicopter
- 2 arrows
- A piece of cake
- A purple balloon
- A parachute
- A dog in a balloon
- A grasshopper
- 3 green fish
- A snail

BALLOON RACE
- 3 star-studded balloons
- 2 elephants
- 2 walking-sticks
- 4 wasps
- A policeman
- An ostrich
- A pirate
- 2 teacups and saucers
- A bird's nest
- A clown

SHOPPING HORROR
- A hammer
- A boy with a radio
- A pink handbag
- A shopper on a skateboard
- A bird in a nest
- 2 red and white bobble hats
- A teddy in a bow tie
- A happy baby
- A pink mouse
- 10 silver coins

SNOWSTORM
- A broomstick
- 15 scarves
- A toboggan
- A bow tie
- 2 saucepans
- 2 twiggy heads
- A red jacket
- 2 top hats
- A pear
- A pipe

TRAFFIC JAM
- A worm
- A clown
- A tank
- A steam engine
- An apple
- A gas mask
- A crash
- A black top hat
- A pink pram
- A radar

CRYSTAL CRATER
- A crystal moustache
- A heart
- 2 hammers
- A stone sculptor
- A stone with a long nose
- 2 chisels
- A stone with matches
- A stone with a black eye
- A stone landing on a stone
- 8 ruby people

ALIEN INSECT SWAMP
- 3 stripy Wally bugs
- A blue snake
- 2 green grass bugs
- A red insect with 3 eyes
- A bug with sharp teeth
- A long purple tongue
- 2 black furry eyes
- 7 yellow bird bugs
- A four-eyed green bug
- 6 one-eyed flies

WALLY LOOKALIKE
- A spider
- A Wally superhero
- An invisible Wally
- 4 striped balloons
- A crocodile
- A fish in a bowl
- A clown
- A ball and chain
- 11 brown walking-sticks
- A flying bee

ANSWERS

CARNIVAL CHAOS — Page 7

Riddle: The green balloon with the clown face is floating behind the strongman.

The code reads: The supersonic rollercoaster.

Misfit: Giraffe from Traffic Jam.

BALL SPORTS — Page 8

Riddle: The man at the front has put his finger through the hole in a table tennis bat.

The pool ball and tennis ball.

The sports are: basketball, football, tennis, swimming, golf, baseball, snooker, volleyball. Swimming is the odd one – it's not a ball sport.

Misfit: Ribbon from Monster Carnival.

MAGIC MAYHEM — Page 9

Riddle: A woman has been sawn in half under the huge pink rabbit.

Silhouette E matches the bunny.

Misfit: Light bulb from Light Fantastic.

FILM SET — Pages 10–11

Riddle: The prop is a white piano underneath the text.

The names are: Sinbad, Aladdin, Mowgli, Tarzan, Dracula, and the piece of equipment is a clapperboard.

Misfit: Space baby from Star Gazing.

MONSTER CARNIVAL — Page 12

Riddle: There is a pink monster with a mushroom hat riding a unicycle.

Ball F is slightly bigger.

B and D are from this page but A is from Light Fantastic and C from Ball Sports.

Misfit: Little hooded man from Ball Sports.

PILLOW FIGHT PARTY — Page 13

Riddle: He is the chap with a big grin near the bottom left-hand corner.

There are 11 pillows in the heap.

The things in the bedsock are: biscuit, book, torch, flea, tissue, glasses, earplugs, mouse.

Misfit: Snake from Snaky Games.

FILM SET FROLICS — Page 14

Riddle: The man Tarzan is looking at is about to step on a banana skin.

The film words are: 1. Screen 2. Camera 3. Makeup 4. Cinema 5. Script 6. Lights.

The kangaroo head is from Crazy Cars.

Misfit: Sunbather from Surfer's Paradise.

TOYSHOP TROUBLE — Page 15

Riddle: There is a small penguin sitting right behind the whale.

C is the piece which has stayed the same.

The across words are: dice, mane, four, duck. The down words are: ball, bear, doll, kite.

Misfit: Pink face from Cream of the Cakes.

MOON WALKING — Page 17

Riddle: There are 14 little green men hiding in the picture.

The planets are: Mercury, Pluto, Saturn, Uranus, Jupiter, Mars, Earth, Venus, Neptune.

```
N E V O Y A G E R I
L A N R M S T R O N
M G A W A S T H E F
E I S R S T M A N O
R N A T L A N T I S
C D I S C O V E R Y
U T H A P O L L O E
R E R O L P X E M O
Y K I N T U P S O N
```

The space fact is: Neil Armstrong was the first man on the moon.

Misfit: Messy face from Fabulous Food.

INVENTION CONVENTION — Pages 18–19

Riddle: A square egg is being held by the scientist next to the robot.

Balloon – Flag A (France) – 1783
Aeroplane – Flag E (USA) – 1903
Satellite – Flag D (Russia) – 1957
Train – Flag C (Great Britain) – 1804
Clock – Flag B (Germany) – 1500

The crab is from Wacky Water Fun and the light is from Shark Shambles.

Misfit: Sea Captain from Wacky Water Fun.

STAR GAZING — Page 20

Riddle: The little martians are in a yellow spacecraft just above the big green planet.

The signpost says: Welcome to outer space.

Misfit: A balloon from Balloon Race.

CONSTRUCTION CHAOS — Page 21

Riddle: He is the man wearing the knight's helmet.

The 6 six-letter words to do with building are: cement, hammer, window, planks, pillar, ladder.

Misfit: Flying man from Carnival Chaos.

FLYING SAUCERS — Pages 22–23

Riddle: To the left of Wally's spaceship is a spaceman floating upside-down who has dropped his ice-cream.

The constellations are: Corvus – the crow, Taurus – the bull, Cygnus – the swan, Leo – the lion, Ursa Major – the great bear, Orion – the hunter.

Misfit: Pilot from Monkey Mischief.

LIGHT FANTASTIC — Page 24

Riddle: Man cooking a sausage over a lamp.

Lamp D is missing from the picture.

Misfit: Space car from Flying Saucers.

RAMSHACKLE ROBOTS — Page 25

Riddle: There is a girl hiding inside a robot suit in the bottom right-hand corner.

The robot's leg is his own.

The values of the letters are: O = 2, R = 3, T = 5, B = 1, so R + O + B + O + T is the same as 3 + 2 + 1 + 2 + 5 which makes 13!

Misfit: Girl from Beach Delights.

SHOPPING SPREE — Page 27

Riddle: He's looking for a slice of cheese next to the man with a cold.

Wally wanted to buy: A Big Chocolate Cake.

Misfit: Top hat from Magic Mayhem.

A FEAST OF PIES — Page 28

Riddle: He's an icing-sugar man, sitting between two sets of steps.

Grains: barley, oats, wheat, millet, rye.

Misfit: Bowl from Ice-Cream Party.

FABULOUS FOOD — Page 29

Riddle: There is a large pumpkin just beneath the right-hand picture.

Bits A and D complete the plate.

The vegetables are beetroot, cucumber, tomatoes, mushroom, potatoes, radishes. Radishes and tomatoes can be seen in the picture.

Misfit: White dog from Dog Days.

CREAM OF THE CAKES — Page 30

Riddle: Two little cakes are sitting on an éclair.

E is the correct piece.

The doughnut ingredients are: old socks, fish hook, half worm, dynamite, fried egg.

Misfit: Chocolate drop from Silly Sweets.

ICE-CREAM PARTY — Page 31

Riddle: The most popular flavour is banana and marmalade.

The ice-cream flavours are: parsnip, broccoli, tomato, cabbage and carrot.

The pudding pairs are: strawberries and cream, pancakes and syrup, jelly and ice-cream, bananas and custard.

Misfit: A fish from Deep Sea Diving.

VEGETABLE MATTERS — Page 32

Riddle: He is a red chilli pepper.

The red pepper, the yellow pepper and the tomato are fruit.

A potato, an onion and an apple are hidden and they take you to letter C.

Misfit: Hat from Mushroom Magic.

EASTER PARADE — Page 33

Riddle: There is an artistic bunny on the hen.

B is the correct bit of shell.

Misfit: Tiny bird from Forest Fun.

COOKING COMPETITION — Page 34

Riddle: The boy on the left has taken a slice of cake.

Misfit: Scarf from Snow Sculpting.

SILLY SWEETS — Page 35

Riddle: The jelly bear is being carried off by the balloon.

Sweet F has the largest surface area.

Misfit: Striped cube from Toyshop Trouble.

WATER WONDERLAND — Page 37

Riddle: There is a message in a bottle on the rock in the middle of the picture.

The coded message reads: To Wally, do come to tea. Love Octopus.

Misfit: Spaceship from Moon Walking.

SURFER'S PARADISE — Pages 38–39

Riddle: He's a teddy bear in Dracula's coffin on the far right of the picture.

The key and the anchor are the odd ones out because they do not float.

If you follow all the instructions you should end up in the Pacific.

Misfit: Fish from Water Wonderland.

WHAT A WRECK!   Pages 40–41

Riddle: He's the mischievous crab sitting on the rock ledge on the right.

The pairs are: crab and shrimp (hard shells), squid and octopus (boneless bodies), the two empty shells, anchor and cannon (found on ship), and the treasure chest and coin.

The treasures you can bring out are: key, chest, ring.

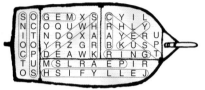

Misfit: Crystal from Crystal Crater.

POOLSIDE PARADISE   Page 42

Riddle: He is the waiter shooting between the columns carrying the drinks tray.

The only piece which matches exactly is E.

The 6 things found in the pool are: watch, banana, boot, sandwich, wig, trunks.

Misfit: Stripy egg from Easter Parade.

BEACH DELIGHTS   Page 43

Riddle: He is the white dog sleeping under the cowboy.

The 7 differences are: bridge of glasses, bows on cap, top of cap, spots on 2nd leg (counting left to right), shape of 3rd foot, bumps on 4th leg, spots on 5th leg.

You find the way from sea to sun like this: SEA, see, bee, bed, bud, bun, SUN.

Misfit: Boy from Poolside Paradise.

SHARK SHAMBLES   Pages 44–45

Riddle: There is a football floating in the water.

The 3 fish are: EAB, FIG, CHD.

The letters read: Dolphins sometimes gang up on a shark and attack it.

Misfit: Scientist from Invention Convention.

WACKY WATER FUN   Pages 46–47

Riddle: He is the small boy standing in the middle of the pool.

The 12 changes are: starfish's eyes, boy's cap, the woman has lost her tan, spots on fish, new starfish in water, stripe on man's trunks, man's open mouth, starfish smile, man's teeth lined, whale's eyes, a scroll, stripes on starfish's float.

The animal pairs are: penguin and seagull (birds), sealion and otter (mammals). The odd one out is the alligator (reptile).

Misfit: Yellow flowers from Jungle Gym.

MUSHROOM MAGIC   Page 49

Riddle: There is a red mushroom with a green cap holding a watering-can.

B, D and E are on this page, A is from Vegetable Matters and C is from Forest Fun.

Misfit: Creature from Ludicrous Leprechauns.

LUDICROUS LEPRECHAUNS   Pages 50–51

Riddle: A pair of scissors cutting giant clover.

Put one coin head-side up on one side of the line, one coin tail-side up on the other, and balance the third coin on its edge along the middle of the line.

Misfit: Coin from What a Wreck!

FOREST FUN   Page 52

Riddle: He is the knight hanging upside-down from the tree on the left.

A and G are the matching helmets.

The first code reads: I've had enough! Let's get out of here!

The second code reads: He has a gold helmet with an orange feather.

Misfit: Slipper from Pillow Fight Party.

DRAGON RIDE   Page 53

Riddle: There is a yellow key just above the dragon's head.

Hunter B has a different moustache, Hunter C has a different hat and Hunter E has different hair.

| MEDUSA |
| MERMAID |
| SATYR |
| PEGASUS |
| UNICORN |
| MINOTAUR |

Misfit: Dinosaur from Dinosaur Games.

MUSHROOM-MINING TROLLS   Pages 54–55

Riddle: The masked marauder is up on a beam in the top left-hand corner.

A and D are on this page, B comes from Wild West Heroes and C from Pirates Ahoy.

Misfit: Choking man from Pirates Ahoy.

CUPID CHAOS   Page 56

Riddle: The tortoise and the hare are in the bottom left-hand corner.

This square is exactly the same as the original:

The saying in code is: Elephants never forget.

Misfit: A snake from Snake Pit.

GREEN FOREST GAMES   Page 57

Riddle: There is a yellow duck standing on the tree house.

The trees are cedar, yew, redwood, spruce, chestnut, poplar, sycamore, beech, willow, oak, and the tree museum is an arboretum.

Misfit: Helmet from The Vikings.

CAVE RAVE   Page 59

Riddle: The mammoth is about to tread on a drawing pin.

The letters left over spell Mad Rock Street.

Misfit: A cake from A Feast of Pies.

MEDIEVAL MAYHEM   Page 60

Riddle: The rolling-pin is falling from the battlements on the far left of the picture.

D is the odd picture out.

Misfit: A tiger from Cave Rave.

VIKING PARTY   Page 61

Riddle: He is the running man with his clothes on fire.

C is the piece which completes the shield.

Picture pieces: A and D are on this page, B comes from Carnival Chaos and C from Jungle Gym.

Misfit: Hard hat from Construction Chaos.

PIRATES AHOY   Page 62

Riddle: The pirate's name is Flora and she's swinging from the rigging.

As for the treasure: It's in the crow's nest.

Misfit: Birds from Film Set.

WILD WEST HEROES   Page 63

Riddle: There is a vase just about to drop from the saloon.

Rope D will unravel the villain.

The pickaxe is the odd silhouette. It can be found in Mushroom-Mining Trolls.

Misfit: A top hat from Snowstorm.

THE VIKINGS   Pages 64–65

Riddle: A Viking is cleaning the helmets on the head of the long boat.

Helmet C is the odd one out.

The dragon is from Surfer's Paradise and the chicken in a spacesuit is from Moon Walking.

Misfit: Child's face from Crazy Cars.

TROJAN ELEPHANT   Page 66

Riddle: A man at the front has been hit.

I escaped using a ladder!

WALLS
SPEAR
SHIELD
SOLDIER
SIEGE
FIRE

Misfit: Hat from Shopping Horror.

ARMOURED KNIGHTS — Page 67

Riddle: He is the knight in yellow armour plummeting from the sky.

There are 12 shields in the pile.

Misfit: Shield from Wally Lookalike.

JUNGLE GYM — Page 69

Riddle: There is a white monkey hanging from the trees by his tail.

D is the hummingbird's shadow.

The snake has swallowed: puma, tree frog, alligator, fire ant, tarantula, tapir.

Misfit: Girl from Viking Party.

SNAKE PIT — Page 70

Riddle: The yellow snake is on the floor in the middle of the picture.

Snake A is the longest.

There are 9 different snakes – adder, boa constrictor, cobra, grass snake, anaconda, rattlesnake, viper, asp, python.

Misfit: Mushroom from Mushroom-Mining Trolls.

DINOSAUR GAMES — Page 71

Riddle: There is a tennis ball in the nest by the purple, sleeping dinosaur.

The daft dino is made up like this:
beak and crest – Pteranodon
head – Triceratops
neck – Apatosaurus
legs and body – Tyrannosaurus
sail – Dimetrodon
tail – Stegosaurus

Misfit: A bird from Cupid Chaos.

MONKEY MISCHIEF — Page 72

Riddle: There is a man with a knife and fork and a potato up on the left.

Plane C matches exactly.

The animals are: tiger, mouse, zebra, camel, whale, horse, chimp, panda, sheep, hyena.

Misfit: Explorer from Film Set Frolics.

DEEP SEA DIVING — Page 73

Riddle: There is a submarine in the bottom left-hand corner, just above the treasure chest.

The seahorse differences are: nose, horn on the head, tongue, back fin, bottom fin, tail.

STARFISH
NET
SCROLL
SHELL
HOOK
TREASURE

Misfit: A diver from Medieval Mayhem.

JURASSIC HIGH-JINKS — Page 74

Riddle: A tortoise is surviving a dinosaur attack at the front of the picture.

The 7 differences between the dinosaurs are: teeth, head crest, extra spine on back, spot on neck, spot on back, tail tip and claws on back foot.

Misfit: Orange alien from Alien Insect Swamp.

DOG DAYS — Page 75

Riddle: There is a little green rule book at the top of the page.

SPANIEL
DOBERMAN
LABRADOR
SHEEPDOG
ALSATIAN
TERRIER

Misfit: Little girl from Shopping Spree.

BIRD BRAINS — Page 76

Riddle: He is the sleepy bird with black wings near the middle of the picture.

E is the piece of shell which completes the broken egg.

The birds are: starling, penguins, flamingo, vultures, nuthatch, buzzards, canaries.

Misfit: Purple dinosaur head from Jurassic High-Jinks.

SNAKY GAMES — Page 77

Riddle: There is a purple vampire snake in the middle of the picture.

The 7 differences are: eyelid, stripe on tie, shape of nostrils, number of teeth, spot near ground, spot on tail, number of lines on tail.

Misfit: The devil from Cooking Competition.

SNOW SCULPTING — Page 79

Riddle: He is the snowman on the bottom right with 3 squashed tomatoes on his head.

The green glove and the radish do not appear.

The flying saucer is from Ramshackle Robots and the scroll is from Easter Parade.

Misfit: Cauliflower from Vegetable Matters.

SHOPPING HORROR — Pages 80–81

Riddle: A blue hairbrush by the dinosaur.

The carrot and the paper hat cannot be found in the picture.

Wenda must buy these things in this order: skirt, teddy, bat, cake. This is her route:

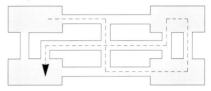

Misfit: Bandana from Trojan Elephant.

CRYSTAL CRATER — Page 82

Riddle: A grey stone with a hole, at the back.

The pairs are: A and J, B and F, C and K, E and H, G and I. The odd one out is D.

JADE
DIAMOND
MARBLE
SAPPHIRE
COAL
OPAL
GOLD

Misfit: Spaceship from Ramshackle Robots.

CRAZY CARS — Page 83

Riddle: There is a baby in a blue pram next to the orange hippo.

Misfit: Bird from Green Forest Games.

SNOWSTORM — Page 84

Riddle: There is a snowman with his head on upside-down, just under the text.

A, B and E complete the snowhead.

Misfit: A boot from Wild West Heroes.

ALIEN INSECT SWAMP — Page 85

Riddle: There is a small orange bug near the middle of the picture who is hanging on for dear life.

A beetle collector is a coleopterist.

C is the shadow of the alien bug.

Misfit: Tiny insects from Bird Brains.

BALLOON RACE — Pages 86–87

Riddle: He's a frog and the number on his balloon is 28.

The highest number is 747.

Picture C is the odd one out and can be found in Film Set.

Misfit: A mouse from Dragon Ride.

TRAFFIC JAM — Page 88

Riddle: He's a dog and he's riding a motor scooter.

The matching cars are A and E.

Find your way from BUS to CAR like this: BUS, BUT, HUT, HAT, CAT, CAR.

Misfit: Film roll from Shark Shambles.

WALLY LOOKALIKE — Page 89

Riddle: He's the purple zebra.

D is the correct stripe.

Misfit: Helmet from Armoured Knights.

AND FINALLY

Woof appears in Film Set, Flying Saucers, Jurassic High-Jinks, Shopping Horror and Crazy Cars.

Wenda is in Easter Parade, Crazy Cars and Wally Lookalike.

Wizard Whitebeard can be found in Magic Mayhem, Film Set, Vegetable Matters, Armoured Knights and Crazy Cars.

Odlaw is lurking in Beach Delights, Viking Party and Crazy Cars.

The striped sock is in Cave Rave and the Wally flag is in The Vikings.

The scrolls are in Film Set Frolics, Construction Chaos, Cooking Competition (2), What a Wreck!, Poolside Paradise, Shark Shambles, Wacky Water Fun, The Vikings, Dinosaur Games (3), Monkey Mischief, Deep Sea Diving, Bird Brains, Snow Sculpting and Traffic Jam.

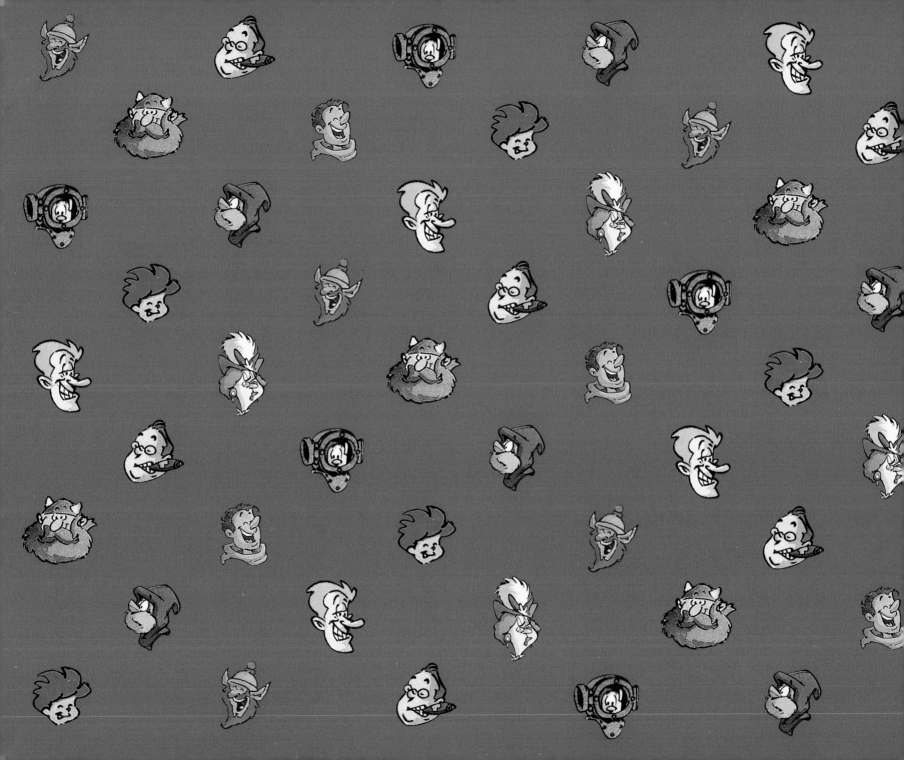